Read what business owners, media executives, and advertising professionals have to say about Michael Corbett's
"The 33 Ruthless Rules of Local Advertising."

"The $E=MC^2$ of local advertising! Michael Corbett and his partner Dave Stilli are, without question, the ***leading experts*** on this subject."

> – Edward Rogoff, Ph.D. – Professor of Entrepreneurship, Baruch College, City University of New York

"This book is a ***must read*** for anyone interested in seriously growing a business. Our business could not have made the great strides we have in ***such a short time*** without applying Michael Corbett's advertising strategies."

> – Clare and Walter Baum, Owners, Baum Diamonds, Chapel Hill, North Carolina

"Your book's format is quick reading and easy referencing. [It] helps advertisers see through all the smoke and mirrors. I wholeheartedly recommend it to everyone…except my competition, of course!"

> – Susan Leeds, Advertising/Marketing Coordinator, Seaway Food Town, Inc., Maumee, Ohio

"I know this book works. It's a fantastic step-by-step guide to successful local advertising. No one has a better formula—period!"

> – Neal Newman, Executive Vice President, Enterprise Media

"More than anything else, I've been exposed to, [this book] has provided a solid basis for understanding and utilizing my advertising in a much more effective manner."

> – Les Akers, Automobile Dealer, Tallahassee, Florida

"Author Michael Corbett *seems to state the obvious*, but the obvious is what many companies forget in their haste to reach the public."

"The 33 Rules teaches business owners like me how to focus our advertising efforts to achieve maximum results. Corbett also approaches advertising by discussing the "real issues" in a way that we business owners (after all, we're not marketing experts) can understand."

– Jay Mashaw, Owner, Moto Photo, Richmond, Virginia,

"Makes more sense than anything I've heard in 26 years in business—from any source."

– Patrick Tachuck, Business Owner, West Palm Beach, Florida

"Read it…before someone else does!"

– *Radio Ink* Magazine

"Over the last twenty years, I've personally worked with thousands of advertisers—large and small—in markets of all sizes, and never met a single one that couldn't benefit from "The 33 Ruthless Rules." If you're operating a business in the next millennium, you'd better have three things at your disposal: a competent accountant, a good lawyer, and Michael Corbett's book."

– Phil Zachary, Radio Station Manager, Washington, D.C.

"Some of the most clear and common sense advice on advertising I've ever seen. If space or broadcast advertising is in your marketing mix, you need The 33 Rules!"

– Shel Horowitz, Author of *Marketing Without Megabucks: How To Sell Anything On A Shoestring*.

The 33
Ruthless Rules
Of
Local Advertising

Michael Corbett

The 33 Ruthless Rules of Local Advertising

Pinnacle Books, Inc.
New York, NY

The 33 Ruthless Rules of Local Advertising

Copyright © 2000 by Michael Corbett

ISBN 0-9667383-9-X
7 8 9 10 11/04 03 02 01 00

Printed in Canada

Published by
Pinnacle Books, Inc. New York, NY
800-285-3210

e-mail: pinbooks@worldnet.att.net

Distributed by
Independent Publishers Group
(312) 337-0747

This book is also available
on Audio Cassette

Table of contents

Part Six Common Sense Marketing

Acknowledgments

David Stilli: Contributing Author

Dave's experience and brilliance on the subject of local advertising are on every page of this book. We've been partners for many years, learning together and applying what we've learned to our own business and to the businesses of many others. That's why you'll see "we" instead of "I" throughout. I am very grateful for his contributions.

Michael Corbett

Special Thanks to:

Jack Mayer for book design and editing
James Stagnitta at JS Graphics, Aurora, Colorado
The Staff at Independent Publishers Group, Chicago
Thomas Leonard at Coach University

And, of course, we are most grateful to our family members and friends to whom we owe so much for their personal and professional contributions.

Michael Corbett
David Stilli

Powerful advertising and marketing on the local level is as critical to the success of a business as dynamite is to gold mining. If you place the dynamite in the right places in the right amounts at the right times, you get a different result than if you are misinformed or under educated about dynamite and you continuously misuse it. You might make a few holes or dents just by making the attempt, but you probably won't get close to the gold, and you may go broke trying.

This book will not have every answer to every advertising and marketing question or circumstance, but it will get you closer to the gold.

Dedication

To all the courageous men and women struggling to make their entrepreneurial dreams come true in an unforgiving marketplace.

And to the memory of:

**Paul Corbett
Steven Sonntag
John Stilli
Newt Rothbart
O. A. Fine**

The vast majority of new businesses will fail in their first two years. Most of the survivors, despite their potential, will barely get by, suffering chronically low profit margins. One essential difference between a business that fails or is perpetually anemic and one that survives and prospers, is how successful they are with their marketing and advertising.

This book was written with the intention of taking the mystery out of advertising for any local business, from the small entrepreneur to the large retailer.

Local advertising can be made to work for almost any advertiser, if certain rules are followed. The local advertising rules in this book are "ruthless" because if you break them, especially those concerning what we refer to as the Real Issues of local advertising, you can lose your business. Like mountain climbing, bungee jumping, and Arctic exploration, local advertising can be tough going even when you follow the rules. But if you break them, the rules are rudely, sometimes mortally, unforgiving.

What makes local advertising so perilous is the fact that the rules for winning in advertising on the local level are not widely known or followed. Most local ad agencies and media sales reps are trained to follow *national* advertising rules and approaches, and that's where the trouble begins. Large national advertisers can *spend* their way out of a bad campaign or can afford to test five different approaches before settling on one. Few, if any, local advertisers have that same luxury. The national advertiser has an army of experts to guide him. These highly trained and thoroughly educated advertising professionals know how to make the rules of national advertising work. They are paid well and have a large pool of financial and technical resources from which to draw.

Local advertising professionals may be highly trained as well, but most operate under one set of broadly-defined advertising and marketing rules. That set of rules, which may apply to the national advertiser, simply does not address the unique needs of the local advertiser.

Most people in the local advertising profession don't talk about *measurable growth objectives* or *absolute accountability*, which are two of the Real Issues of local advertising.

Over the years we have purchased millions of dollars of local advertising. When local media sales reps first called on us, we would ask them four Real Issues questions:

◆ **Now that you've told me how much you want me to spend with you, could you please tell me how much of a measurable growth objective or gross sales objective I should set for that expenditure?**

◆ **How long will it take to reach my growth objective?**

◆ **What system of absolute accountability can you put in place to show me that your plan is working, besides asking people— who don't really know anyway— what brought them in?**

◆ **If I hit the objective, how will I know your plan was responsible?**

The 33 Ruthless Rules of Local Advertising

2

We never found a sales rep, media sales manager, or ad agency who could satisfactorily answer those questions. The words "measurable growth" and "absolute accountability" don't mix well with the word "advertising."

You'll find the answers to those Real Issue questions in this book.

In over a decade of conducting advertising workshops and seminars, we have found that less than 10% of the business owners who attended were consistently satisfied with the results of their local advertising. In virtually every case in which their advertising was not consistently profitable, they were breaking some or all of the 33 Ruthless Rules of Local Advertising.

We've had the privilege of working as an advertising adviser to many businesses who, after unfailingly applying the Ruthless Rules, began to realize far greater satisfaction with their advertising results.

We acknowledge that not all of you who read this book will have the capital necessary to advertise in your local marketplace. For those of you to whom that applies, the section on Common Sense Marketing can be used to stimulate the growth of your business and provide an advertising budget. But the tenets in that section apply to any business, even those with a considerable advertising budget.

To appreciate how each of the Ruthless Rules and the Common Sense Marketing tenets work together, we recommend that you read the entire book before implementing any of them.

Michael Corbett
David Stilli

The term "customer" refers to someone who already spends money with you (as opposed to the browsing shopper you refer to when you say to a sales clerk, "go wait on that customer.").

A "prospect," "prospective customer," or "shopper" is someone who has yet to make a purchase.

"Consumer" means either or both a prospect or customer

The word "advertising" relates strictly to the use of the local mass media.

What we mean by "marketing" (as in Common Sense Marketing) is absolutely anything even remotely related to the promotion of your business, and even includes things like behavior and attitude.

While advertising is literally a part of marketing, it is a very distinct part, and has been from its inception. It shall remain distinct on these pages.

The 33
Ruthless Rules
of Local Advertising

Part
ONE
Setting Up To Win

Advertising Is Neither A Necessary Evil Nor A Cure-all

Many businesses stop advertising in slow times because they consider advertising little more than a necessary evil that may or may not be useful. Other businesses think all they have to do to increase business is to advertise. Neither of these viewpoints is productive.

Effective advertising can produce and maintain steady growth in any economic circumstances. That growth is relative. By "relative" we mean between 10 and 30 percent more growth than a non-advertising, similarly sized competitor, or 10 to 30 percent more than a competitor who is advertising ineffectively.

A restaurant owner we worked with was experiencing a flat sales curve from the previous year. After some research—it's surprising what you can learn from vendors—we found out that his primary competitors were down about 20% from the same period in the previous year. In essence, our client was holding a steady sales curve in an economy that was down 20%.

That's what we mean by relative growth. It's all relative to (primarily) local economic conditions.

Build A Rock-solid Marketing Bridge

People will perceive your business the way your marketing represents your business.

The marketing bridge is made up of whatever links you to your customers and potential customers. That means **everything**, from the way you answer your phone, to the clothes you wear, to the color of your building. Everything you do or have done to attract and keep customers is part of the marketing bridge. Given that definition, almost every recommendation in this book is in some way connected to the marketing bridge, but the specific parts or "elements" of the marketing bridge we'll be referring to in the first five sections have a direct, though not exclusive, connection to local advertising.

The marketing bridge comprises many elements, all of which must be strong and solid before you advertise or advertise any more. Spending money on advertising before you address your marketing bridge needs is very risky. It's risky because you might be unknowingly sabotaging your own advertising efforts. A weak marketing bridge element can turn away a potential customer, and sometimes the potential customer doesn't even know why he or she is uneasy about doing business with you.

Here are a few internal and external marketing bridge elements to consider:

Telephone

Too many companies never put themselves in the consumer's shoes. If they did, they wouldn't allow their phone receptionist to make it so difficult for consumers to do business with them!

Does your receptionist or whoever answers your phone have the same commitment to your customers that you do?

Can the person answering your phone make a compelling response to the caller's requests?

Have you told your phone receptionist, or anyone who answers your phone, that 83 percent of effective phone communication occurs in the tone of voice?

Does he or she answer your phone no later than the third ring?

How much training has the person(s) answering your phone had in taking care of people who call your business?

Do they like talking to people? Are they smiling when they communicate on the phone?

Do they consider people who phone with questions or complaints a bother, an interruption, a pain?

How is your receptionist perceived by your customers?

Don't take for granted that you already know the answers to these questions. Investigate. If you find that you have people who aren't or who can't be superb on the phone, don't let them answer it. They're doing serious damage to your business that you may not even be aware of.

Employees

The actions of your employees are essential to high repeat and referral business

percentages. Good employees, therefore, are an integral part of your marketing bridge, and the success of your advertising results will, in large part, depend on them.

How well trained are your salespeople? How much time have you spent with them preparing exchanges, phrases, questions, alternatives, and advice to offer or ask your shoppers? How willing are you and your people to answer questions or offer important advice to the consumer, even advice that may not even benefit you at the moment?

Do your employees get the sense that they count, that they're important to you, that they makes a difference?

Are your employees enthusiastic about what they do or are they just going through the motions, waiting for the clock to move?

Are your employees authentically acknowledged by you or your managers regularly?

What's usually missing in businesses with morale problems is a sense of purpose, accomplishment, counting, importance, contribution, or of making a difference. These are all basic human needs, and if you're an employer who can fulfill them, people will want to work hard to please you.

Business Name

Does your name say what you do? Does it connect in any way to your product/service? See if you can tell what these (real) businesses sell:

K-9 Corral
Surf and Turf
Hoof and Paw

13

Give up?

K-9 Corral is a jeans shop.

Surf and Turf is a bedding store.

(They sell waterbeds and conventional beds. "Surf" for the waterbeds they sell and "Turf" for the conventional beds they sell. Plus, as the owners explained, they give away a steak and lobster dinner with each purchase! It seemed to make perfect sense to them.)

Hoof and Paw is a boutique.

If your name is as confusing to people as these are, make fun of it, try to make sense of it, but don't ignore it. Either change your name or make a direct issue of it in your ad copy.

Years ago we worked with a store named Eclectic International when the word "eclectic" was anything but familiar to most people. It was obvious that unless the problem with the name was addressed, no amount of advertising would be effective.

My associate and we took a tape recorder to a busy, local mall and asked passers by, "What is Eclectic International?" We wanted to use the answers we got in a radio campaign designed to introduce Eclectic International to local consumers and to handle the name problem as well.

The copy went something like this:

Announcer: *Welcome to What's That Business. I'm asking people the question: "What's Eclectic International?" How about you ma'am?*

Woman: *Don't they make zippers?*

Announcer: *And you sir?*

Man:	*I think they're underwear manufacturers, aren't they?*
Announcer:	*You sir?*
Man:	*That's where I pay my light bill, right?*

These were real answers from real people!

Eventually we had to put a ringer in the crowd who'd give us the right answer ("it's a furniture store, right?") and bells would ring and sirens would wail and we'd give a "prize" of incredible selection and value to anyone who'd remember that Eclectic International was a furniture store. We then explained the meaning of "eclectic" and how the name fit the multinational inventory, and so forth.

This approach went on for a few months and the ads were so successful that they not only introduced a furniture store to the market in a way that made the store memorable, they also introduced a word to the market. The results were dramatic, but they wouldn't have been without first addressing the obvious problem with the name.

Location

If you have an undesirable location or you're difficult to find, address that in copy. Again, don't ever ignore this or any obvious marketing bridge problem. "We're not easy to find. We did that on purpose so you'd have something to talk about besides all those great values we're gonna give you when you get here."

Store Visibility

Are you easily seen from the street? If you aren't you'll have to address it in copy. Don't make it even harder for consumers who may not know that you're tucked away in the corner of a mall or off the beaten track. Let them know, head on.

Signage

This is a made-up word but not a made-up problem.

Municipal codes and other circumstances may limit the size or location of your exterior signs. If it's a real problem, don't ignore it—"If you can find us with our tiny sign, you've got better eyes than most humans and a lot better chance at getting some of the best service in the solar system."

What about interior signs? More than 70% of all purchase decisions are made right on the premises! Point of purchase signs can be creatively designed to get the attention of the buyer at a low cost to you.

Inventory

Do you carry what's hot or what's not? Are your inventory levels adequate? Is your inventory well displayed and easily found?

Parking

Is it adequate, convenient, accessible, well marked? If not, are you addressing it in copy?

Prices

Are they higher than, lower than, or competitive with your primary competitors?

Service

Providing your customers with excellent service is simple. Not easy, but simple. It's also cost efficient. *It will cost you six times more to get a new customer than it will to keep one.* If you aren't a service maniac, you had better be prepared to spend a lot more for the same results than someone who is serious about service. A service maniac will have a very high repeat and referral percentage while a business offering average service will be turning over customers continually.

Become paranoid about service!

Quality

Is the quality of your goods/services as good as, better than, or the same as your primary competitors?

Image

Is it excellent, good, fair, poor? Why?

Name Recognition

Is it high, average, low, non existent? If you asked a hundred people in your target market "who do you think of when you think of (your type of product/service)," how many would say your name?

General Customer Perception

Repeat and referral business will be decided by the way your customers perceive

17

your ability to satisfactorily fulfill their needs. How do your customers or prospects perceive your business?

Marketing Materials

Are the materials you use to represent your business doing their job? Are your brochures professional and easy to read? What about your inventory displays? Is your store clean and neat always? Do your stationery and business cards look great?

Advertising

While advertising is only one element in the marketing bridge, it is certainly one of the most critical, because advertising is the most conspicuous connection you have with the consumer community.

Effective advertising will influence perception and attract consumers to your business, but only a rock-solid marketing bridge will produce the growth that comes from repeat and referral business. That is to say, if there are elements in your marketing bridge that are weak, those same customers you attracted with your advertising could be lost forever.

The Next Step

There are three actions you can take right now to begin strengthening your marketing bridge:

1. From the following list of marketing bridge elements, select those that pertain specifically to your business:

    Company purpose/vision
    General customer perception
    Telephone

Employees as responsible "partners"
Business Name
Location
Store visibility
Signage
Inventory
Parking
Prices
Service
Quality
Receptionist
Image
Name recognition
Marketing materials
Advertising

2. Grade the elements that pertain to your business on a scale of 1–10 (1 meaning fatally weak, 10 meaning rock-solid).

3. Capitalize on the marketing bridge elements that grade the highest, and begin to fix those elements that grade poorly. If those that grade the weakest are not fixable, don't ignore them, address them head-on in your advertising copy.

Compile An Accurate Profile Of Your Customers

If you don't do so already, you *must* find a way to obtain and record accurate and updated information about your existing customers. The information you gather should include:

Age Range:
   Majority between _____ and _____,
   most others between _____ and _____

Gender (%):
   Male _____ Female _____ Couples _____

Income Category:
   Majority between $_____ and $_____,
   most others between $_____ and $_____

Employment Category (%):
   Blue Collar _____ White Collar _____ Professional
   _____ Ethnic _____ Urban _____ Suburban _____

Proximity to business (%):
   Under 5 mi. _____ 5-10 mi. _____ 10-20 mi. _____
   Farther _____

If you need help in compiling an accurate customer profile, ask for the market research conducted by your vendors for their products, or do some in-store research with the cooperation of your employees. Except for "income," where the best you can do is take an educated guess, you can gather all of the other information called for in your customer profile.

Identify Your Target Market

Who do you want to reach with your message?

Usually a business will want to reach prospects with the same profile as its existing customers. A dress shop that attracts younger women between the ages of 18 and 25 will normally want to advertise to women of that same age range. So the first step is to get an accurate profile of your existing customers. Once you've done that, it's just a matter of targeting prospects who fit that profile.

An exception to this would be if you were a new business and didn't have an existing customer profile. Another exception might be if you were introducing a new product or service that would not be applicable to your present customer base. In both those instances you will have to conduct some industry sponsored research on formulating a target market or you'll have to get some input from someone who has the experience to target your advertising, like the owner of a similar business in another market.

Warning: resist the temptation to be all things to all people. If you're a jewelry store that has found a niche in your market by being known as a specialist in diamond engagement rings, stay strong in your niche. In other words, don't decide that the success you have built in your niche will naturally allow success in another niche, like gold watches. It's expensive enough trying to advertise to one target market, let alone two. Businesses that have tried this fragmentation targeting almost never succeed.

If you don't have a niche in your market among your competitors, find one, and then build on it (See Rule 9).

All The Advertising You Can Afford, Isn't Worth The Customers You Already Have

Major corporations want information about their customers. For example, they'll induce you to send back a warranty card that's filled with questions about you and your family. In addition to selling your name to mailing list companies, corporations use that information to do several things:

♦ **They make decisions on advertising and marketing based on that information.**

♦ **They make future product decisions based on what they learn from you.**

♦ **They contact you to sell you another of their products.**

The point is, if they get no information *from* you, they have no contact *with* you. If they have no contact with you, they have no opportunity to re-sell you (make a similar sale), cross-sell you (sell you ancillary goods/services), or up-sell you (sell you a more expensive product/service).

Your existing customers are your best prospects for re-selling, cross-selling or up-selling.

Computerize your customer profiles for purposes of database marketing. Then put the information you have about your customers to use, much as a national company does. Having the ability to contact your customer base through direct mail several times a year can allow you to make several additional sales per customer that you would have not made otherwise.

We recently worked with a single location clothing store owner who had about ten thousand customers per year, but who had no database, and thus no preferred customer mailing list. This business had a $35 average ticket and an average of about six tickets per customer, per year. He was grossing about $2,100,000.

We exhorted this business owner, as we would all business owners, to formulate a database of customer information and to keep it accurate and updated. We then showed him how to create a mailing piece with special purchase inducements.

Each ten thousand pieces, if mailed every other month for twelve months, would cost about $5,000, or a total of $30,000 yearly. If, from the six mailings, this advertiser got just one additional average sale from each customer, he would gross an additional $350,000. That's an additional 16% of present gross sales before doing any other advertising!

This preferred customer mailing piece would produce a lot better results than the conservative objective we set for this advertiser, but even if it bombed and produced only half of the sales objective, it would still be a great investment.

There are any number of occasions for staying in touch with your customers via

direct mail. You can mail to preferred customers for special events or sales, or offer them a private sale. Just make sure the customer sees the content of your mailing piece as a legitimate, motivating opportunity and not another piece of junk mail.

Having and using a database is more than a good idea. It could be the difference between making it big or not making it at all.

Know What A New Customer Is Worth To You

This is not an easy evaluation to make, but it's a critical one if you're going to manage your advertising expenditures with any degree of accuracy and justification.

By determining the value of a new customer, you can decide how much to invest to acquire a new customer through advertising/marketing.

To calculate the value of a new customer, begin by knowing the value of an existing customer.

1. **What does your typical customer spend on each purchase (average ticket = gross sales ÷ number of sales)?**

2. **What's your net profit on an average ticket (gross sale less cost of goods/services less advertising costs)?**

3. **How long does your typical customer patronize your business (patronage lifetime)?**

4. **How many purchases does your typical customer make over his/her patronage lifetime (repeat sales)?**

5. How many prospects will your typical customer refer to your business in his/her patronage lifetime (referral sales)?

6. How often will that customer base turn over (how many new customers will you need to replace those who will leave, and over what period of time)?

7. What have you spent to get the customers you now have (cost per existing customer)?

8. Taking the net profit per sale (gross sale less the costs for goods/services and advertising), times the number of patronage lifetime sales, and factoring in any referral business that may come from a new customer, what is a new customer really worth to you? Is a new customer worth one average sale? 100 average sales? More?

After making these calculations, you may see that you will be spending more to get a new customer than the amount you realize from the new customer's first purchase. But you may also come to the conclusion that the future profits from that customer may more than compensate for the initial loss.

Understand The Purpose Of Advertising

Do you advertise to "bring people in" or to "keep your name before the public?" Advertising can and should be much more specific, more exact:

The purpose of advertising is to create an equity position in a target market and to reach and motivate a sufficient number of consumers so that a business can realize a specific growth objective.

(An *"equity position"* in the context of advertising is when people think of *your business* when they have a need for the product/service you sell. **The** equity position in a market would be when the consumer thinks of your business **first**.)

The objective of advertising is to first have an impact on the mind of the consumer followed by or accomplished simultaneously with an impact on the spending of the consumer. As you can see, that's just about the opposite of the way most local advertisers think. Most local advertising is aimed at one thing, which is motivating a consumer to buy *right now* through price consideration. The ads center on spending, but they almost never take equity position into consideration.

The Rules that follow will pertain to fulfilling the purpose and objectives of advertising.

Set Measurable Growth Objectives

There are two primary reasons for setting measurable growth objectives for your advertising:

1. **You'll know exactly how many additional prospects you'll need on a daily basis to hit the growth objective.**

2. **You'll have a way to hold your advertising expenditures absolutely accountable.**

The first step in setting a measurable growth objective for the advertising budget is to collect certain information.

Average Ticket

Your average sales ticket is determined by dividing your gross sales by the number of sales over a given period, in this case the previous 12 months. (Set aside abnormally high and low tickets to get a more accurate working average).

Closing Percentage

Out of ten prospects who come in or who phone you, how many will end up buying, even if they come back or phone back more than once before making a purchase? If it's three out of ten, your closing percentage is 30%. (You may need some help from your employees in getting an accurate closing percentage. If you go to your employees and ask them to keep track of how many customers they sell vs. how many they talk to, they may skew the results in their favor, out of fear that you're keeping tabs on their sales ability. We recommend that you truthfully tell your employees that you are implementing an advertising effort that requires accurate feedback for accountability purposes. Tell them you need their assistance to get the information you need. Make your request to them as non-threatening as you can.)

Average Daily Floor Traffic Count

Take the total number of sales for the past 12 months and divide that answer by the closing percentage you arrived at. That will give you your annual (or past 12 months) floor traffic. Divide your annual floor traffic count by 12 for a monthly floor traffic count. Divide your monthly floor traffic count by the number of days you're open per month for an average daily floor traffic count.

Estimated Number of Direct or Major Competitors

If you think you have no competition, ask yourself if you're doing 100% of the business in your field? If not, who is taking some of the pie? Whoever's sharing the pie is a competitor. If you look in the yellow pages, will you have the sole listing in your category or associated categories?" If not, whoever else is listed is a competitor. The

bad news is that you have competition, like it or not. The good news is most of your additional prospects—thus your growth—will come from pulling prospects away from your competitors. The more competitors, the more prospects available. The more prospects available, the more growth available. Again, a good way to determine the breadth of competition is to look in the yellow pages and see who sells the same or similar goods or services. What about department stores, super stores, or any other type of business that might carry your goods or services? Make a list of all your competitors. That list will be helpful later when you have to formulate how many additional prospects are available.

Your Competitors' Estimated Daily Floor Traffic

This isn't too easy to determine, but try to estimate which competitor is bigger than you, smaller than you, or about the same size as you. Then assign a floor traffic number to each, as an estimate. This is not a critical factor in determining your advertising directions, but it is interesting to see how many prospects are not yet coming to your business.

Total Daily Prospects Available From Competitors

Add up the floor traffic counts of each competitor to get a broad idea of average daily number of prospects shopping for your product or service.

We're now ready to set a growth objective of between 10 and 30 percent (for most businesses) above anticipated gross sales for the next 12 months. This is the amount that advertising is responsible for producing, above what you might have produced if you had changed nothing.

> NOTE: If you're a new business, you'll set a "gross sales" objective instead of a growth objective because you have no sales history, thus no sales trends for the past few years. A new business will also likely have an erratic sales curve in the beginning years. Your gross sales objective will be determined by research that tells what you should achieve in the way of gross sales in the early years. You'll use advertising to support that gross sales goal and eventually add to it.

Let's use a fictitious business to show you how to set a growth objective:

Acme Jewelers is a one location jewelry store in mid-America. Acme looks in his yellow pages and lists 19 viable competitors. Some competitors bring in six prospects per day. Some have thirty prospects or more, depending in their size, location, and how many years they've been in business.

All of the competitors together average 15 prospects per day.

Viable competitors:	19
Estimated floor traffic/competitor:	15
Estimated total daily prospects:	285
Gross sales past 12 months:	$620,000

Acme Jewelers

Gross sales (12 months):	$620,000
÷ Number of sales (tickets):	1937
÷ Closing percentage:	30%
= Total prospects (12 months):	6456
÷ 12	
= Average monthly floor traffic:	538
÷ Days open per month:	26
= Average daily floor traffic:	20.6

Once we get the annual sales figure, we use division all the way down the next table to figure the average daily floor traffic count:

Acme has looked at local and national trends for the jewelry business. Its annual sales curve has been fairly predictable at about 10% per year for the past few years, and it expects to achieve about the same percentage of growth in the next 12 months.

Acme is also a candidate for a 10-30% additional increase over its expected growth just by advertising effectively.

Acme's projected gross sales for the next 12-month period is $682,000 (the $620,000 grossed in the past 12 months plus 10% expected increase). Now we'll set a growth objective.

The growth objective will come strictly from effective advertising. Acme can expect to gross about $682,000 if they do nothing different, because its sales history had demonstrated that it will grow by about 10 percent per year. But effective advertising should be able to produce an additional $150,000 (about 22%) over and above its $682,000, for a gross sales total of $832,000.

What will it take to get this additional $150,000?:

Growth Objective Analysis

Growth objective:	$150,000
÷ Average ticket:	$320
= Additional number of sales needed:	469
÷ Closing percentage:	30%
= Additional Prospects needed (12 months):	1563
÷ 12	
= Additional prospects needed per month:	130
÷ Number of days open per month (26)	
= Additional prospects needed per day:	5

Acme now knows it will require 5 additional prospects per day to realize its growth objective. And, by incorporating the 33 Ruthless Rules of Local Advertising, Acme is now perfectly positioned to achieve its objective and beyond.

Part

TWO

Gaining
The Advantage

Use The Single Most Powerful Tool In Local Advertising

It's called a **Unique Selling Proposition or Preemptive Advantage**.

What is it that you have or do that your competition does not have or cannot do? By answering that question you'll be finding a Unique Selling Proposition (**USP**) or a Preemptive Advantage (**PA**). You'll also be finding a way to *position* your business relative to your competitors. (See Rule 17)

A Unique Selling Proposition or Preemptive Advantage is some outstanding feature or benefit that people can associate or identify with your business, and yours alone. It becomes synonymous with your business. A **USP/PA** is something you develop after looking at your competitors and seeing what's not being offered that you can offer. It might be a feature of your industry that none of your competitors is talking about, a feature of interest or importance to the consumer.

A USP/PA distinguishes you from your competitors. (It can even be something that produces a *perception* of uniqueness. Are you really better off being in the good hands of Allstate? If people think they are, who's to argue?)

You can do on a local level what advertising great Claude Hopkins did on a national level. In the 1920's Hopkins, a brilliant ad man, was asked to visit the home of Schlitz beer in Milwaukee. This was at a time when Schlitz was not yet a household name and not yet "the beer that made Milwaukee famous."

Hopkins was given a tour and was fascinated by what he saw. He noticed that although the brewery was just a few hundred yards from Lake Michigan, the water used by Schlitz came from several deep, artesian wells. He saw brewing rooms with glass windows several feet thick and rooms where beer was repeatedly tested. Hopkins then saw the room where hundreds of yeast "recipes" were created until the perfect yeast, the "Mother Yeast," was formulated for the beer. He saw how the beer bottles were washed several times before being filled.

When the tour was over, Hopkins asked the Schlitz executives why they weren't showing off these fascinating, unique brewing processes to the public. He was told, "The truth is, every brewery does about the same thing. We're not unique."

Maybe Schlitz wasn't unique, but Hopkins noted that though every brewer might use the same techniques, not one of them was talking about it! So he developed a campaign to educate the public about how they did things at Schlitz. The public didn't know that every brewer used virtually the same process to manufacture beer. And, when they were told about the perceptually "unique" brewing approaches at Schlitz, Schlitz became a top ten beer seller for the first time.

Few local businesses have developed a Unique Selling Proposition/Preemptive Advantage. In fact, most aren't even aware of the idea. But a business without a Unique Selling Proposition/Preemptive Advantage is a

business among businesses, just another store front. With a USP/PA you have an advantage you can capitalize on time and again.

One more note on the USP/PA. It can't be stated as a cliche or time-worn phrase. It might be true that you have "the lowest prices in town" or "the best service in the city," but you can't use those words to say so. Those are phrases everybody uses and nobody believes. They've become hackneyed, worn and impotent. You have to find a way of communicating your USP/PA so that it doesn't go unheard or unseen.

For example, if your USP/PA is being a "discount house," instead of saying "We have discount prices," say something like, "Try this price out anywhere else...$500 TV's only cost $399 at Jones TV and Appliance..." That statement backs up your USP/PA without resorting to the usual cliché-like language of "lowest prices," etc.

If Your Doors Are Open, You Should Be Advertising

There are five indisputable reasons to advertise all the time:

1. People Shop All The Time

You're not advertising to a standing army. You're advertising to a passing parade.

Different people are shopping all the time for the goods or services you sell, and they'll buy those goods or services from you or from your competitors. If you want a bigger share of the consumer market, you have to let people know about you. You do that by advertising all the time.

2. People move

As much as twenty five percent of your market is mobile each year. Each time a household in your area replaces itself, you have a chance to educate and motivate a new consumer. There are always new consumers to educate and motivate.

3. People forget

How many advertising impressions do you remember from yesterday, not counting your own or your competitor's? Ten, five, two, one, none? How many advertising impressions do you think you were exposed to since yesterday? One hundred? Two hundred? How about several hundred to several thousand! Think about it. You received ad impressions by the hundreds when you read the paper, looked at TV or listened to the radio. You also saw billboards, signs on buildings, signs on trucks, signs on uniforms, signs on buses and cabs, signs on bus benches, ads on matchbook covers and pens and pencils. You also got ad impressions from reading your mail and pouring your orange juice.

4. People often take their time before buying

Most people are impulse buyers, but not when it comes to the larger purchases such as appliances, cars, houses, expensive jewelry, and so forth. A consumer can be in the market for a big ticket product or service for several weeks or months before a purchase is made. Your job is to keep yourself out in front of the consumer throughout the buying cycle:

◆ **deciding to shop**

◆ **making final determinations on product, brand, and price**

◆ **actively shopping**

◆ **making the purchase**

If you advertise all the time, you have a better chance of getting the buyer's attention, and their inquiry. If you don't advertise all the time and your competitors are "out there" more than you, they'll probably have a better chance than you to make the sale. If you're both out there, the advertiser with better media schedules and stronger copy will win out more often than not.

Because you don't know when any particular prospect will be in the market for your product/service, you cover yourself when you advertise all the time.

While the previous reasons for advertising all the time are important, the next is critical.

5. To establish an equity position in the consumer community

Remember, an equity position among consumers is: *When someone needs your product or service, they think of you.*

Here are some examples of national companies that have gained an equity position by use of Positioning Statements/Slogans and Unique Selling Propositions or Preemptive Advantages.

When you want facial tissues, what do you put down on your list? Kleenex, of course. But Kleenex is a brand name. There are many different brands of facial tissue but Kleenex has an equity position among consumers. What do you ask for when you want a photocopy of a document? A "Xerox" right? Xerox is a brand name that's become synonymous with photocopies.

What's the game you play with a green, plywood table, a net in the middle, paddles, and small plastic balls? Ping Pong? No, you're playing table tennis. Ping Pong is a brand name that's become synonymous with table tennis.

The objective is this: Get into a consumer's brain and you'll get into his/her bank account.

Another way of saying the same thing comes from the former president of one of America's most heavily advertised companies, General Foods, who said, *"Advertising is that force which gets the share of consumer mind…which must*

47

precede getting an increased share of consumer market." That's quite a remarkable statement when you think about it. He's saying that you have to get an equity position—which can only exist in someone's mind—before being able to count on increases in market share!

As stated before, that's almost 180 degrees from the way most local advertisers advertise. Most local businesses advertise as though the only business to be had is immediate business, and the only way to motivate people to action is to practically give away the inventory.

In other words most advertisers go after the consumer market with no concern for capturing the consumer's mind (equity position).

The way to gain an equity position among consumers is simple: consistently expose three things about you to the consumer community: your **name**, your **location(s)**, and your **Unique Selling Proposition or Preemptive Advantage**.

Budget Adequately For Advertising

By "advertising," We mean primarily the use of the local mass media; radio, TV, newspaper and billboards.

> For our purposes, don't include yellow page ads in your advertising budget. That's a fixed, monthly expense once it's ordered and you have no flexibility with it as you might other media. Also, separate such expenditures as church bulletins, civic calendars, business cards, stationery, and signs, from your mass media advertising budget.

Many businesses determine their ad budgets by some formula. For example, a research report on your industry might state that a certain percentage of sales was spent on advertising over a specific period of time: "Industry X spent 2 percent of gross sales for advertising in the last fiscal year." What was just a report often becomes a rule for local members of that industry. "I only spend 2 percent on advertising because that's what the report says."

While there's nothing wrong with having a fiscal guideline in deciding an ad budget, you'll have to become flexible with that guideline as market demands change. If you're stuck on spending only a certain amount, usually decided by some imaginary percentage figure, or you're stuck on advertising only in certain media, as suggested by a marketing plan provided by your industry, you will also be stuck with whatever results those budgets and media can produce. As a starting point, earmark between 5 and 10 percent of gross sales for advertising. We realize that those percentages are general, and that many businesses will need to budget more or less than 5 to 10 percent of sales, depending on the type of business.

A fast food chain with high gross sales and low margins might budget two percent, while a furniture store with high tickets and high margins might spend as much as twenty percent, on occasion.

However you formulate your ad budget, once you do so, don't forget to include an amount equal to about 10 percent of the ad budget for producing the ads, or making them media-ready.

Think Long Term

How far out do you plan your advertising? Do you have a one year plan? A five year plan? A ten year plan? (The Japanese have a national growth plan that extends for hundreds of years!) At minimum, a local advertiser should have a long term, flexible budget, a Unique Selling Proposition or Preemptive Advantage, and a commitment to at least a 12 month advertising plan.

Short term results can occasionally occur as a result of a heavy schedule of ads in a short period of time. You may get a good turnout for a special event, but you can't count on any kind of consistent results with short term media schedules. Using the media for infrequent, short term advertising schedules will not get you the same growth benefits you'll get when you advertise with consistency, frequency, and impact. If you advertise from week to week, idea to idea, promotion to promotion, you're usually going to end up disappointed.

You might want to begin to look at advertising the same way you looked at your business when you first started it. You didn't say "let's try this business for a month to see how it works," as is often said about advertising schedules. Your commitment to your business was far greater than that.

Ultimately, the media should be used as vehicles for long-term growth, requiring a long-term commitment. Not having an accountable advertising plan, and not staying with that plan, has been a primary reason for failures of local businesses.

Most businesses back off or stop their advertising when sales get slow, then when sales pick up they begin to advertise again. While that may be financially convenient, it can be devastating to a plan for strong, steady growth.

Have A Potent Promotional Strategy

A growth oriented promotional strategy consists of three actions:

1. Informing
2. Persuading
3. Reminding

Informing means getting specific with your target market about what you have or do. It means educating people about your goods/services in a very specific, comprehensive way.

Persuading means stressing the benefits and features of your products/services relative to your competition's benefits or features.

Reminding means consistently repeating certain things, including the benefits and features of what you have or do, in a way that has people think of you when they need what you sell.

The way to inform, persuade, and remind people is to get or to have:

1. **Publicity**: Publicity is a free form of advertising, like press releases.
2. **Sales Promotions**: These are usually internal promotions like sales contests, prize drawings, or point of purchase displays.
3. **Personal Selling**: This is nothing more than you or your customers telling oth-

ers about your business, or "word of mouth" advertising.

4. **Mass Selling**: Mass selling is using the local mass media to inform, persuade, and remind people about your product or service.

Each of these tools can be used effectively to increase your business. Usually, the fastest way to achieve growth is to motivate prospective customers through the use of the local mass media (As presented in Part Four – Managing The Media).

RULE 14

Don't Advertise What You Can't Deliver

A **Unique Selling Proposition or Preemptive Advantage** is not just a slogan or a good idea. It's going to determine the perception and experience people are going to have before and after doing business with you.

Can you live up to the perception your advertising will give customers of your qualities, prices, service, merchandise, conveniences, or selection?

One way to make sure you can deliver on your Unique Selling Proposition or Preemptive Advantage and be consistent, is to train everybody in your company to respect the company's USP/PA. If you can't get agreement from everyone on your company's USP/PA, work on another (or work on getting another staff!).

A Response Is Not A Result

Knowing the difference between response and results will save you fortunes. A great number of advertisers seem to confuse the two, so it's important to clarify the difference:

"Response" is when someone comments on your ads, tells you that you look good on TV, or sings your radio jingle.

"Results" is when they buy something.

Response may make you feel good because people are saying they're hearing/seeing/reading your ads and you're getting the impression that your advertising is working. *Response is very seductive—it feels like results!*

Here are two questions that can help anchor you the next time you get distracted by response:

1. If response means my advertising is working, why are my sales flat?

2. Would it be OK with me if no one commented on my ads but my business grew anyway?

The response is the response.
The results are the results.
The two are not the same.

Don't Ask Your Customers What Brought Them In

The way most advertisers attempt to track results is by asking their customers what brought them in. Allow us to share an experience:

When Michael was getting started in the advertising field, he was responsible for the successful grand opening of a new "lumber" store. This was a complete store that carried almost everything imaginable.

Michael, his boss, and the store owner stood at the front door of this huge place and polled customers as they walked in for the grand opening weekend. As they entered the store, each shopper was asked: "What brought you in?"

Roughly 50% said radio, 30% said TV, and 20% said newspaper. What interested the poll-takers most was the fact that *they never ran an ad on TV*. The grand opening was advertised only on radio and in the newspaper.

How could it be that 30% of the people who came into that store that weekend said they saw the ad where it had never been? And when questioned them about how sure they were, they were *sure*.

After speaking to scores of local advertisers who have had a similar experience when they polled their customers in an attempt to evaluate the effectiveness of their advertising, We've learned some things about polling and about people, and about what not to do with the polling results:

◆ **People don't know what brought them in.**

◆ **People don't know that they don't know what brought them in.**

◆ **People don't like not knowing what brought them in and they want to be helpful, so they'll make things up.**

◆ **Never change your multiple media advertising plans based on what people say brought them in.**

The only foolproof way to evaluate advertising effectiveness is by setting measurable growth objectives for your business, and by monitoring the results in the cash register. Period.

Part THREE

The Magic Ingredient- Copy

Position Your Business

A Unique Selling Proposition or Preemptive Advantage can be effectively expressed in a **Positioning Statement**. Let's say you're a soft drink bottler and you want to position your product relative to your competitor's product. You'd have to find something unique about your soft drink first, then you'd have to communicate that uniqueness in a brief, memorable, catchy way.

One of the most powerful positioning statements in retail history was made by 7-UP as they tried to find a USP/PA with which to battle the colas. It was seven words that changed the soft drink industry. The positioning statement was, *"No caffeine. Never had it, never will."*

Was 7-UP saying that caffeine was "bad?" Was it saying that 7-UP's cola competitors had bad caffeine in their soft drinks? The beauty of this statement was the timing. It was introduced when we were being educated to the ill effects of caffeine. 7-UP never had caffeine, but that fact was overlooked until the health consciousness of America began rising, and the company used it as a Preemptive Advantage.

The result of this marketing coup was that 7-UP suddenly experienced one of the largest market share increases in soft drink history, and forced every major bottler to market a caffeine free drink. Ironically, another soft drink, RC cola, was also caffeine free, but RC didn't capitalize on that Unique Selling Proposition/Preemptive Advantage. 7-UP did.

Continually look for opportunities to position your business relative to your competitors, and then tell your marketplace about it:

...."Bloomington's only 24 hour printer, and we deliver."

...."The sports shop with the largest inventory in three states."

...."Smith's full time florist. We deliver love seven days a week."

RULE

Weak, Sloppy, Boring, Sleepy, Careless, Pointless, Cookie-cutter, Cliché-filled Copy Won't Do!

The media hire salespeople to sell time and space. Don't expect those same people to be copywriters. A piece of copy that sells well might take days to write. A blockbuster head-line alone might take hours to create. Turning your copywriting over to a media salesperson or media copywriter is a huge gamble. We recommend that you study the following guidelines on copy components and learn to write your own copy. If you can't write your own copy, at least learn the rules so you can be your own copy editor.

K.I.S.S.

Keep It Simple, Stupid. That means you have to learn to get your message across effectively without jingles, without humor, and without distracting production. Write your ads to seek sales, not applause. Imagine that every ad is a salesperson working for you. Would you require your salespeople be performers as well? Keep in mind that your purpose is to motivate people and get results, not to entertain them and get response.

In a few instances humor or jingles or an off-beat production may be temporarily successful. A few others may be successful long-term. These are the exceptions! For every ad you remember that was funny and entertaining there are thousands that tried and failed.

Never mention or even allude to your competitors in your ads. If you do, send them part of your bill because they owe you for the exposure you've given them. People don't always pay close attention to ads, and you could easily and unwittingly cause the same consumers you're trying to attract to remember your competitor instead! We know they do this a lot on national commercials, but you're not a national advertiser, you're a local advertiser. You're in deep, dangerous waters when you start mentioning your competitors in your ad copy.

Another dangerous habit is running counterproductive "comparison" ads where you set up a scenario that compares the way you do business with the way your competitors do business. Again, people don't always pay close attention, and they might associate the negatives you're pointing out with the prominent name in the ad—yours!

The Headline Is The Ad For The Ad

Advertising great David Ogilvy said, "On the average, five times as many people read the headline as read the body copy. It follows that, unless your headline sells your product, you've wasted 80% of your money."

How many newspaper ads or radio ads or television ads have you observed, or worse yet, have you actually run without a blockbuster headline or "teaser?"

Here are a few headline hints:

1. Avoid using reversed type (white type on a black background) for any more than a small portion of your ad, if at all. It's harder for people to read the ad and it looks cheap, especially on newspaper pages.

2. Don't use all capital letters. A mix of upper and lower case, like this sentence, is easier to read and looks better THAN ALL CAPS.

3. Keep the headline relatively short, less than 15 words.

4. Make sure the headline is just that, a shortened version of the body copy, a teaser.

5. Headlines can be very effective when posed as a question people want an answer to. ("There Are Two Types Of Consumers, Which One Are You?")

6. Put quotation marks around the headline. You'll get 25% better results.

The Permanent and Variable Copy Elements

There are two basic elements of effective copy for local media: The **permanent** elements and the **variable** elements. The permanent elements are those elements that are always included in each ad. Those elements include your **name**, your **location**, and your **Unique Selling Proposition or Preemptive Advantage**. These are the elements that are designed to create an equity position with Future Buyers.

The variable elements are those elements that can and do change from time to time, such as the price of a product/service or the benefits/features of the product/service. These are the elements designed to attract the Now Buyer. The permanent and variable elements are the superstructure of the ad.

Stay Away From Clichés

Or, as someone once quipped, "Avoid clichés like the plague!"

Most local ads are alike. Almost all are an uninspiring, yawn-inducing collection of time-worn phrases and clichés. "We'll give you fast, friendly service." "We have the lowest prices in town." "Drive a little, save a lot." "We'll beat any deal." "Nobody sells for less." (Did you ever hear of a housing development that wasn't "nestled" somewhere?) "The customer always comes first with us," *AD* nauseam.

People stopped believing those clichés decades ago, but most advertisers act as though they're the first to use those expressions, or something close to those expressions. So the "copywriters" continue to write virtually the same copy for every advertiser.

Let's say you have a Unique Selling Proposition or Preemptive Advantage, like fast service. Whoever writes your copy has to be able to get that USP/PA across without clichés. You have to be able to say "fast service" in a different way. Maybe you can demonstrate your fast service by saying something like: *"We at Sal's Lumber know you're used to standing in line at other stores so we hired more helpers than our competition. We just thought you'd like to get home sooner."*

Now if you put in some prices/items and a location or two, you've given a message that

can be heard. People can't hear clichés but they can be attentive to something unique that says the same thing as the cliché but in different words. The same goes for your print ad.

Blame Sal If You Walked Away Happy!

"We at Sal's Lumber would like to thank those of you who expressed your delight this past weekend for being waited on so quickly. Evidently some of you new customers aren't used to that kind of service..."

Make It Easy For People To Find You

Don't give complicated street directions in copy. Instead, let people know where you're located by giving them familiar cross streets or landmarks.

"We're at route 441 and Howard Blvd," is an example.

"Our brand new store is at 1099 Welby Road, just across the street from the Civic Center," is another.

If you are not located near anything familiar, have people call you for directions, but don't tell them to look you up in the yellow pages. When you tell people to do that, you give them a chance to see all of your competitor's ads as well. Tell them to look for your phone number in the white pages, and tell them how it's listed.

You can use a simple map in print media, but the simpler the better. However, we recommend having them call if it's so difficult to find you that people need a map.

Sell Benefits and Features Equally

Features have to do with the *practical* aspects of your product or service while benefits have to do with the *emotional* advantages your product or service can provide. Although some features could be considered benefits and vice versa, most benefits are distinct from features.

Features: What makes buying your product or service logical? What practical reasons can you give for someone to use your product or service? Will it last longer? Is it fade resistant? Is there a guarantee? What about conveniences?

Benefits: What impact will your product/service have on your prospect's emotions? Will it cause a feeling of well being? Will it produce a sense of joy, happiness, power, love, achievement? Will it create a sense of security and strength? Will it engender contentment, comfort, or peace of mind? What will your product do for the buyer's senses? Does your product/service taste, feel, sound, look, smell like something that will attract people?

Most ad copy appeals to only about half of the people who will see, hear, or read it. Why? Because only about 45 percent of the people reached by your ad copy are motivated by the emotional benefits of your product/service. Another 45 percent are motivated by the practical, logical aspects of your product/service. The remaining 10 percent are attracted to a product or service both emotionally *and* practically.

Hitting the hot button of almost everyone exposed to your ads requires you to write *balanced* copy. Half of the ad should

contain the benefits or "feeling" aspects of your product/service and the other half should stress the practical, logical reasons to buy your product/service. That doesn't mean you have to separate your ad into two distinct segments. You can mix the benefits and features together, just be sure they receive equal emphasis.

If yours is typical of most ad copy, it's not balanced. It's either weighted on the side of emotional appeals or on the side of practicality. The objective is to get all your copy in balance so that everyone you're reaching is attracted by some aspect of it. Before writing your copy, list the benefits and features you'll be including in it. If you see that the features and benefits are not balanced, balance them:

Clothing

Features: On sale, fabric, style, up-to-date, charge it

Benefits: Pride, appearance, envy, compliments

Ring

Features: Value, financing available, good investment, heirloom

Benefits: Joy, beauty, love, pride, envy,

One Idea At a Time

Stick to one theme at a time. Don't mix events or promotions. If you're stressing prices, make prices the main theme. The same with service or whatever else you're stressing at the time. Another theme can be included, but only as a brief aside.

Credentialize

Another aspect of effective copy is credentializing. Your credentials may even be your Unique Selling Proposition or Preemptive Advantage. For example, you're a dry cleaner who specializes in furs and you're specially trained to do that type of cleaning, unlike your competitors. Or you're a carpet dealer who is "industry recognized" for his customer satisfaction ratings.

Identify and include anything that looks like what I've described as "credentializing" in your copy. It's a significant plus for positive consumer perception.

Use The 10 Critical Components Of Copy

Composing your advertising copy can be far less painful or stressful if you use the critical components as a map to get you through the process.

The way to insure the effectiveness of your ad is to make sure it includes all the critical components. With the exception of number ten (below), which may or may not apply, the critical components are as necessary to the success of your ad as oxygen is to fire.

Be advised that the critical components cannot be used when writing copy for all media. You could not, for example, expect to include all the components in your billboard or yellow pages copy. But you can include them in all TV, radio, newspaper, and direct mail.

The 10 Critical Components

1. **A Powerful Headline, if in print, or the "Opening Statement" for electronic media.**

2. **The Basic Story**

3. **The Proposition**

4. **The Exact Offer**

5. **A Guarantee**

6. **A Call To Action–Immediacy**

7. **Your Name**

8. **Your Location(s)**

9. **Your Unique Selling Proposition/ Preemptive Advantage (USP/PA) or Positioning Statement**

10. **Marketing Bridge Elements That Need Addressing**

Numbers 7, 8, and 9 should be included at least twice in electronic and direct mail ads and at least once in newspaper ads.

The following ad, written for a local radio station, contains all but the last of the 10 Critical Components (this advertiser has identified no Marketing Bridge problems):

WE DELIVER LOVE SEVEN DAYS A WEEK! THAT'S RIGHT...AT BIDWELL'S FLOWER AND PLANT SHOP WE'LL DELIVER YOUR GIFT OF LOVE WITHIN 90 MINUTES AFTER YOU ORDER IT OR IT WON'T COST YOU A THING. IF YOU CALL BIDWELL'S FLOWER AND PLANT SHOP OR STOP IN AT 7TH AND BUTLER DOWNTOWN...WE'LL FILL YOUR ORDER OF ANY FLOWER ARRANGE-MENT OR PLANT FOR ANY OCCA-SION...AND WE'LL DELIVER IT WITHIN NINETY MINUTES OR YOU WON'T PAY!

WHY NOT CALL RIGHT NOW WHILE YOU'RE THINKING ABOUT IT? BID-WELL'S FLOWER AND PLANT SHOP AT 7TH AND BUTLER DOWNTOWN DELIVERS LOVE SEVEN DAYS A WEEK...AND NO ONE HAS OUR NINETY-MINUTE DELIVERY GUARANTEE. CALL NOW AT 555-0055 OR LOOK IN THE WHITE PAGES FOR OUR NUMBER UNDER BID-WELL'S FLOWER AND PLANT SHOP.

Let's break this ad down and identify the Critical Components:

WE DELIVER LOVE SEVEN DAYS A WEEK!

(Opening Statement, USP/PA)

THAT'S RIGHT...AT BIDWELL'S FLOWER AND PLANT SHOP WE'LL DELIVER

(Name once)

YOUR GIFT OF LOVE WITHIN 90 MINUTES AFTER YOU ORDER IT OR IT WON'T COST YOU A THING.

(Basic Story, Guarantee, Positioning Statement)

IF YOU CALL BIDWELL'S FLOWER AND PLANT SHOP

(Name second time)

OR STOP IN AT 7TH AND BUTLER DOWNTOWN...

(Location once)

WE'LL FILL YOUR ORDER OF ANY FLOWER ARRANGEMENT OR PLANT FOR ANY OCCASION...AND WE'LL DELIVER IT WITHIN NINETY MINUTES

OR YOU WON'T PAY! WHY NOT CALL RIGHT NOW WHILE YOU'RE THINKING ABOUT IT?

(Proposition, Exact Offer, Guarantee, Call To Action–Immediacy, Positioning Statement second time)

BIDWELL'S FLOWER AND PLANT SHOP

(Name third time)

AT 7TH AND BUTLER DOWNTOWN

(Location second time)

DELIVERS LOVE SEVEN DAYS A WEEK…

(USP/PA second time)

AND NO ONE HAS OUR NINETY-MINUTE DELIVERY GUARANTEE.

(Guarantee, Positioning Statement third time)

CALL NOW AT 555-0055 OR LOOK IN THE WHITE PAGES FOR OUR NUMBER UNDER BIDWELL'S FLOWER AND PLANT SHOP.

(Call To Action–Immediacy second time, Name fourth time)

The sample written for Bidwell's Florist might be very effective if Mr. or Mrs. Bidwell could be their own spokesperson in their ads. Assuming they are capable spokespersons, no one knows or can sell flowers and plants better than Mr. and Mrs. Bidwell.

Here are four easy steps that will help you include the critical components:

1. **Get the attention of your target market in your headline or opening statement.**

2. **Let your target know what you're offering or proposing.**

3. **Develop your proposition with the remainder of the ad and include the reasons why your target should act now.**

4. **Tell your target how and where to find what you're offering.**

A.I.D.A.

This acronym (and title to Verdi's popular opera) might help you in remembering the previous four steps:

Attention

Interest

Desire

Action

If you just remember those four words when you sit down to create your ads, you'll be able to write very effectively. Look at the copy we wrote for Bidwell's Florist, and identify the **A.I.D.A.** as you read it.

One other tip: when you write your copy, think of people singularly, not in the mass, and speak (write) directly to him or her. When you plan your ads, picture a typical customer sitting across from you. Your headline has gotten his or her attention. From then on, let everything you write be guided by what you would do or say if you were face to face with that customer.

The late Joe Karbo, a direct mail genius, offers the following simple, and almost infallible, format for a great mailing piece. The same format can apply to the copy you write for other media as well:

1. Think about the benefits and advantages your product or service will bring to the prospect.

2. Write your best points down.

3. Pick out the singularly best, most powerful, all-encompassing, benefit or advantage. This will be your headline.

4. Your headline should appeal to one or more basic human needs—what he called the 4-R's:

   Reincarnation: The desire for immortality, youth, or vitality.

   Recognition: Acknowledgement, identification, or distinction.

   Romance: Attractiveness, desirability, or popularity.

   Reward: Wealth, achievement, money, or power.

Try to work your product or service into one of those four basic needs and write your piece from there.

Use Advertising's Most Compelling Words

There are certain "buzz" words, when used in print copy or electronic (radio and TV) copy, that seem to get more of the consumer's attention. Our advertising industry has, over the past several decades, "trained" consumers to react positively to these words. When you sprinkle your copy liberally with these words you'll be upping the odds of winning.

Here's a list of advertising's most compelling words:

you	easy
results	benefits
free	sale
money	startling
save	yes
secrets	discovery
fast	safety
health	guarantee
new	how
revealed	proven
why	now
love	

Always Get Two Prospects For The Price Of One

In Rule 8, we set a growth objective for Acme Jewelers that would require an additional 5 prospects per day to walk through Acme's doors. Just how realistic is it to persuade those additional five prospects?

Acme has estimated that their competition is getting a combined 285 prospects every day. We'll call these 285 people the "competitive pool" of prospects. These prospects are also called *"Now Buyers"* because these people are in the market to buy right now.

There's another pool of prospects who are not shopping right now but who might be shoppers sometime in the next few months. These are called *"Future Buyers."* These people could become Now Buyers at any time.

To persuade the Now Buyer pool to act in your favor now, and to prepare the Future Buyer pool by gaining an equity position, two distinct sets of information must be given in the same ad copy. We covered some of this previously, but it bears repeating:

Permanent Ad Copy Elements

Insure long term growth by informing, persuading, reminding, and gaining an equity position with the Future Buyer. This gets accomplished with the repetition of your

name, your location(s), your Unique Selling Proposition or Preemptive Advantage, the permanent elements in copy.

The objective with the permanent elements of copy is to make sure that when future prospects join the Now Buyer pool of shoppers, they do so with the name of your business in mind.

Variable Ad Copy Elements:

Get immediate growth when you motivate the Now Buyer with a price/item value or a promotion that practically obliges them to shop at your store. You do this with the variable elements in copy.

The objective with the variable elements of copy is to attract whatever business you might have otherwise lost to a competitor. This is done by forcing immediate attention.

If Acme jewelers writes unique ads that contain the elements we just described, and if they schedule their ads as directed in later Rules, Acme will certainly motivate an additional five prospects from the huge pool of Now Buyers and Future Buyers.

Here's the magic formula: by *consistently* reaching sufficient numbers of prospects in both prospect pools a *sufficient* number of times, you will be advertising with the impact necessary to motivate a few additional prospects daily.

Again, *reaching a sufficient number of prospects a sufficient number of times* is the key to successful advertising, *assuming you have mastered writing ad copy.*

Part
FOUR

Managing The Media

Understand The Objectives Of Media Salespeople

Over the past thirty years, we have both been media reps, worked with media reps, managed media reps, employed media reps, or trained media reps. We haven't trained just a few—but *hundreds* of media reps. We've trained media reps for radio, television, and even billboard companies. We're telling you this so that you know we have some experience with what we are about to assert:

Media salespeople are trained to sell their inventory, not your inventory.

Once you absolutely understand that, you'll be in a position to use the media more effectively.

Having said that, we hasten to add that the majority of career media reps care about the success of their clients (you). They care not only because it makes a difference to their income, but they care because each of them enjoys the feeling of satisfaction that comes with being told by their client that they did a good job or made a difference.

We want to make it clear that we're not knocking media salespeople when we talk about their training or, more to the point, their lack of training, in moving your inventory.

One result of the demands to perform which are put on media salespeople by their owners and managers, is that many media salespeople are not building a career, they're building a *month*.

The directives from their superiors are, "write business, hit budget this month, sell our inventory now!" And how do they spell job security? (Insert your name here)

Media reps are trained to discuss rates, ratings, packages, promotions, formats, size, color, locations, placement, "free" cruises, and going to lunch. But most media reps are not familiar with, nor do they ask the questions having to do with advertising's Real Issues:

◆ **Are your gross sales satisfactory?**

◆ **Is your advertising producing consistent results?**

◆ **Is there growth available in the marketplace for your business?**

◆ **Is there a way to determine and justify your advertising budget?**

◆ **Can you identify and correct anything in your marketing bridge that's getting in the way of your advertising success?**

◆ **Is there a formula you can use that will produce dynamic ad copy?**

◆ **Is there a way to set a measurable growth objective for your ad budget?**

◆ **Is there a certain way to use the media to gain an equity position and measurable growth?**

◆ **Is there a simple system of absolute accountability that allows you to determine the effectiveness of your ad expenditures?**

If media reps were trained in the importance of *accountability*, they'd be discussing the Real Issues, not distractions like ratings, cost efficiency, and "free" trips or other inducements.

(Question: Why does a medium have to offer incentives to an advertiser if what they are selling works as well as they say it does? You'd think that if the media could consistently deliver on its promises or implied promises, they'd be getting free cruises from you advertisers!)

Media reps are told to establish a "relationship" with their clients. It is assumed that if media reps have a "relationship" with you, you'll learn to like them and buy their inventory in honor of that relationship. Rather than a relationship with media reps, what you really want is "relatedness" with media reps. *"Relatedness" occurs when the media rep and you are both related to the same objectives—yours!*

Media salespeople are not trained to understand the *business* of advertising, they understand the *selling* of advertising. They are not trained in local marketing, they are taught to sell time or space.

When a sales rep from any of the media first called on one of us, we would quickly determine if they were trained to sell their inventory or ours by asking four "Real Issues" questions:

1. **Now that you've told me how much you want me to spend with your medium, could you please tell me how much of a growth objective or gross sales objective I should set up for that expenditure?**

2. **How long should the growth objective period be?**

3. **What system of accountability can you put in place to show me that your plan is working, besides asking people—who don't really know anyway—what brought them in?**

4. **If I hit the objective, how will I know your plan was responsible?**

As we said, we've never spoken with a media owner, manager, sales rep or ad agency who could satisfactorily respond to those questions, and we've never spoken with an advertiser who wasn't vitally interested in the answers.

We liked and admired several of the media reps who called on us. Some of them have been close friends of ours for many years. But once our prospective advertising roles were defined—we'd do the buying, they'd do the expediting (but no selling)—we would relegate the media salespeople who called on us to a position of coordinator and valuable service provider. We would tell them what we wanted and they would expedite our needs. It was a relationship that worked profitably for all parties.

For media people reading this who may take exception to our assertions about their training:

How can you explain why more than 90% of the local/advertisers we've worked with are not happy with their advertising results? Until media owners, media managers, and media sales reps can counter that 90% statistic, there's something very wrong somewhere.

And even if that 90 percent figure was 25 percent, it would still warrant a red flag. In the meantime, we again assert that more than 90 percent of the advice, the copy, and the schedules being proffered by local media reps are not consistently doing the job for the advertiser. Otherwise there wouldn't be the appalling turnover of clients and salespeople in local media. It's a safe bet, based on statistics, that fully 60 percent of the advertisers who were advertising on or in a particular medium 12 months ago are not doing so now. And it's an equally safe bet that 50 percent of the media salespeople who called on a small to medium sized advertiser 18 months ago are now gone.

If you doubt our facts, why not conduct your own satisfaction poll? Ask your present advertisers and former advertisers from the past two years if they're satisfied with the results they get from their advertising efforts? See what percentages of satisfaction you come up with.

As for you local advertisers: your best chance for success in the world of local advertising, where few experts reside, is to learn all you can about the use of each medium, about how to schedule your ads, and about how to write your own copy. *If you can't learn to manage your own advertising (or find someone to help you who can follow The 33 Ruthless Rules), you can't hope for much success with advertising on the local level.*

Any Medium Will Work If You Know How To Work The Medium

Let's examine the local media one by one:

NEWSPAPER

The way newspaper salespeople sell is "bigger is always better." But research conducted by the newspapers themselves have revealed something different. The research (Daniel Starch Report) reveals that in a large number of retail categories:

- ◆ **A full page ad will provide a very small percentage of increased reading, seeing, associating or noting of your ad, versus a half page ad, but you pay twice as much with most papers.**

- ◆ **A half page ad will provide only a slightly larger percentage of increased seeing, reading, associating, or noting of your ad versus a quarter page ad, but you pay twice as much with most papers.**

- ◆ **Adding color to your ad provides a very small percentage of increased reading, associating, or noting your ad, but you pay a premium for color.**

Even without research, common sense and experience shows that the newspaper is more of an information medium for Now Buyers, than it is a motivational medium. In other words, people will read, see, note, or associate your ad at a time when they are already motivated to buy, but seldom before that.

We could say that the newspaper can be described as a price and item catalog for the Now Buyer. It's a place for shoppers to compare prices and information *after they've already been motivated to buy*.

Once a buyer has been motivated, and looks through the newspaper, he or she is doing so to find a specific item and to compare prices. The Now Buyer will almost always find your ad, even if it's not a full or half page.

The readers of most newspapers are middle aged and older, and wear white collars. If you are looking for buyers under the age of forty, you will find fewer of them by advertising in the newspaper than in other media.

For those Now Buyers who do read newspapers, the reading of the ads is usually the final step before shopping at your business. Before that, something motivates a prospect to begin the shopping process. It could be immediate need or it could be the creation of a need through the influence of the motivational media (radio–TV). Then the prospect who may read the newspaper looks at your ad and your competitors' ads for price comparisons and for other information.

Finally, the prospect comes into your business. You may then ask the prospect what brought them in. The prospect remembers the last thing he or she saw was the newspaper ad and says "the ad in the paper." With this comment, you assume the newspaper brought them in.

What the buyer forgot is what started the whole process in the first place, which was motivation by need or by other media. So maybe what you should be concentrating on is *what motivated the buyer to read the newspaper ad in the first place!*

Immediate need or the electronic media is where the buying cycle usually begins. Therefore, the electronic media will be used to create immediate need and to establish your *equity position*.

The managers of heavy newspaper advertisers, like car dealerships, usually think newspaper is the most effective form of advertising. If you ask them why, they say that people come in to the dealership all the time carrying a newspaper with one of their classified ads circled. After reminding them that people won't carry in a TV or a radio or a billboard, ask them what they think motivated their buyers to look at the newspaper ad in the first place. Remind them that the newspaper research says that a very small percentage of readers ever read the classified display section, where the car ads are. Those readers are almost all Now Buyers! There are few browsers in classified display.

After musing a bit, they'll come to realize that people read their car ads because they were either in need of a car or were persuaded by another medium that they "need" to trade cars.

Once you understand that the few motivated buyers who read car ads read them carefully, no matter what size the ad, you are then in a position to save large amounts of money. You can (and many advertisers have) reduced their ad sizes and newspaper budgets by as much as 50 percent, while maintaining or increasing sales.

One other note to car dealers and all those who advertise in the same section or on the same day: *never advertise outside the section where all your competitors advertise!* People are used to looking there for car ads and will not respond the same to yours if it's a maverick ad in some other section. Buyers want to see the cars and prices or all the grocery ads all in one place so they can do their comparing. Why make it inconvenient for them, and why exclude yourself from the comparison process?

The newspaper has been the traditional medium for many local businesses. For centuries it was the only medium. But most consumers don't rely on the newspaper as much as they once did. They get their motivation and information from many sources.

The readership ages have changed; buying habits and priorities have changed; media choices have changed. The only thing that hasn't seemed to change is the tradition of thinking that the newspaper is still the motivation source for most consumers. It clearly is not. That role has been taken over primarily by TV and radio, either of which consumers spend much more time with than they do newspapers.

(One of the most expensive, wasteful, pathetic sights in advertising is a size/color/frequency battle among local competitors. The biggest winner in those wars is always the newspaper.)

Newspapers can be used to inform a price conscious Now Buyer, once that buyer has been motivated by other media or by an immediate need for your product or service.

Newspapers, in our experience, are neither appropriate nor affordable as your

primary vehicle for domination or impact. The greatest strength of the newspapers might be their very useful role as a support for your primary vehicle for domination of the media.

As with other media, repetition and frequency are keys to advertising success in the newspaper. For many businesses, several smaller ads placed throughout the paper may be preferable to one large one.

Another important note: if you want to make your print ads work better, dominate the electronic media. Use those media to draw attention to your newspaper ads. ("Look for our ad in Tuesday's Beacon.")

Commercial Television

Television has been without question the most powerful, most influential medium ever invented. It has been a very successful advertising vehicle for local advertisers. It is unique, in that it alone provides sight and sound and color and motion.

It used to be—and may still be in some cases—that by the time you paid for effective production, there was little left for air time. This was especially true if you changed your ads often, *which is imperative*. But television stations are faced now with shrinking revenue streams, especially outside the top 30 or so television markets. Network affiliates are getting less compensation for carrying network commercials; 30 percent less in some markets, even more than that in others.

There are more television stations now than at any time in history. When you add the scores of channels available through cable systems, it becomes clear that *your* advertising dollars are critical to the survival of those stations. That's good news for you as a local advertiser, in that your bargaining power will inevitably increase as competitive realities take hold among local TV stations and cable systems. You can get ads produced at a reduced cost—and sometimes at no cost at all—with the purchase of a consistent schedule.

People do not watch television *stations,* they watch television *programs.* If you are targeting a particular type of consumer, especially a narrow target like women 25-49, you may have to buy ads on more than one station in several different programs each week to reach your target audience in sufficient numbers.

Consistency is the key to equity position and subsequent growth. Using TV as your primary vehicle for domination, which means you'll be advertising with frequency, consistency, and impact, will require asking your TV rep for a schedule that has your ads on the air a *minimum of two weeks per month every month of the year.*

Your objective in those two-week flights is to reach a minimum of seventy percent of your target market with a frequency level of three net impressions. That means that each of at least seventy percent of all the viewers in your target demographic will see your message at least three times during your two-week run, and probably more. These are minimum impact levels.

If you use TV, it will be either your *primary* or *secondary* vehicle for domination. The type of schedules you buy must depend on your target demographic and whether

your schedule is designed for impact (primary vehicle) or for support (secondary or backup vehicle).

As a consistent TV advertiser who is using TV as a primary vehicle for domination, and as part of your two weeks per month schedule, it is possible to expand your reach and to maintain minimum frequency levels while buying popular prime time weekly programs. Your job, with the help of your TV rep, is to determine which programs best match the demographic and psychographic profile of your most profitable prospect and then to buy as many of those same programs as your budget will allow.

Generally speaking, however, the programs that allow you to build frequency quickly are those that air daily. These would include local news, syndicated shows that run during the hour before the news (early fringe), or those shows scheduled during the hour just before network prime time (prime access). Also included in the daily program fare are network daytime programs. Use those programs mainly for support schedules (i.e., for your special events).

If you're using TV as support for other media, such as radio or direct mail, you'll be buying TV only on occasion, and mostly for special events. Ask your local TV rep to formulate a schedule that will begin at least three working days before the event's start date. At a minimum this schedule should reach at least seventy percent of the target demographic at least three times per viewer. The larger the event in scope, the more time, reach, and frequency you'll need.

The construction of your TV ads, as with all other types of ads, can make or break your objectives. An effective TV commercial does not have to be expensive, and it should not be made with the goal of winning a local "Addy" award (why don't they ever have an award for "most gross sales produced?"). In fact, the most effective local TV ads are those that are straightforward, utilizing simple production techniques. In television, the more time the station (or private production facility) spends on your production, the more expensive it will be.

For those of you who have the money, produce your ad on film. Film is ten times warmer, far more professional looking, and different from what most local advertisers use, which is video tape.

Cable Television

Several cable systems now offer the ability to buy air time on selected channels, but in many markets you have limited choices on where and when your commercials will run. Also, at this time some cable systems do not have local insertion equipment and have to rely on out of market companies to run your commercials via a network setup. In this instance you may have to provide the cable company with a one week lead to change your copy, and you may not be able to pick your programs, channels, or times.

Many cable systems sell their air time on a basis of twelve, eighteen, or twenty four hour rotating time slots, with little or no choice of programs.

While the cost of a cable ad appears at first to be inexpensive because of the unit rates, this medium can also be the most expensive to buy in terms of people reached per dollar expended. Here's why: in most markets, only 60 to 70 percent of the households subscribe to cable,

so your message will not be seen by 30 to 40 percent of all households. On top of that, an average of 70 percent of all cable viewing is to the local TV stations that are carried on the cable. That means that only 30 percent of all the viewing on cable is to non local cable channels, and the 30 percent who are viewing non local channels are watching an average of eight cable channels. Obviously those viewing habits severely fragment the total viewership and diminish the viewership totals per channel.

In short, when you buy time on your local broadcast TV station, you're automatically reaching most of the cable viewers and those viewers who are not on the cable. Buying only a cable schedule will restrict your reach severely and increase your relative costs dramatically.

Having given you the statistics and drawbacks to the use of cable systems, let us now state that it is possible to use cable in a way that can work for your business. If you choose to use cable, *make sure the cable system allows you to buy specific programs, times, and networks.* e.g.:

25 commercials that will run Monday through Friday between 7 p.m. and 10 p.m. on CNN only.

Or:

5 commercials per week, Monday thru Friday, on the Larry King show.

Some cable system ad reps will tell you that you can make a buy as described above, but that it will cost you a "premium." If that premium is more than 30% higher than their base rate, we recommend you put your money elsewhere. The audience levels for specific programs are usually not big enough to justify more than a 30% premium.

As for the production of your cable ads, few cable systems have the production facilities to provide you with a good, competitive ad. You may have to have your ad produced by an outside production house. Though often more expensive, paying for outside production is preferable to letting a poor quality cable system ad represent your business.

Billboards

Billboard advertising has two primary strengths:

1. **Boards can be effectively used to introduce a new product or service to the marketplace with a heavy, short-term showing.**

2. **Boards can be used to provide directions to your location, especially if you're difficult to find.**

The two most important words you can put on a billboard are *NEXT EXIT*. If you can't get a board location where "next exit" applies, try for one where you can say "one mile ahead," or some other simple direction.

It's almost never appropriate to use billboards as a primary vehicle for domination, given that board inventory is generally too expensive for that purpose. If you do buy billboards, here are some guidelines:

◆   **Billboards are too expensive to use as a major part of a growth campaign, but**

they are very useful as a "location" reminder.

◆ **If you do find a use for a board make sure you have only one, large graphic and no more than six words with clear, large type.**

Radio

Radio is the quintessential, "let's try it for a week and see how it works" medium. That's generally the way it's bought. The way it's generally sold is with the impression that short term schedules will get impressive results, but it doesn't always work that way.

Radio has been historically confusing to buy because of the large number of stations available in most markets, each promising the same things: "we're number one, we have the best cost per point, the best rates, the greatest packages, better promotions, happier clients, "free" trips to the Bahamas," and so forth.

None of those issues is as important as results. If you can't or don't buy radio for its strengths, you're just as likely to get poor results on the number one station as you are the lowest rated station, and at a much higher cost.

Like television, radio is primarily a motivational medium, but can be informational as well, like newspapers.

Many radio stations are affordable enough to use as a primary vehicle for domination. Many advertisers have done so with great results. Here's what we mean by "dominate" a radio station:

To dominate a station or stations you have to buy schedules that give you a frequency level of three to five net impressions per week, each week for the first sixteen weeks, and three weeks out of four weeks thereafter. The terms "net impressions "and "net frequency" refer to the number of times the majority of the listeners in your target demographic will hear your commercial in the course of a week.

Not all radio stations are alike. The number of commercials you will need to reach the listeners in any given daypart, such as 6:00 a.m. to 7:00 p.m. or 10:00 a.m. to 3:00 p.m., is dependent upon the amount of time your target demographic spends listening to that station. If people listen longer to a radio format such as Country Music, you can reach those listeners three times net per week with fewer commercials, in this case let's say 12 or 15 commercials per week, Monday through Friday from 6:00 a.m. to 7:00 p.m.. Those 12 or 15 commercials will reach enough people enough times to create an equity position in about twelve weeks and motivate people to action (increase your floor traffic) within thirty days from the time your schedule begins.

People tune some radio formats in and out more often than others, such as News/Talk or some Rock formats, so you may have to run 20 or 25 commercials per week in the same time period to reach your target listeners three times net with your message.

The radio stations have the information (usually computerized) to determine the number of commercials you'll need in any daypart to get a net weekly frequency of three.

If you're a small advertiser who can't afford a schedule of 12 to 25 commercials per week, but you want some frequency and consistency, run one commercial per hour between midnight and 6:00 a.m. It will be dirt cheap and you'll even reach sufficient numbers of listeners to grow, although at a slower pace. Your growth objective will have to be smaller, but you'll get a good start. We have a friend who started a jewelry store chain by advertising just on certain radio stations between midnight and 6:00 a.m. The stations didn't have many listeners in that time period, but they had a sufficient number of listeners to grow, which was the key.

Another way to be a dominant advertiser on radio is to choose your station and then run several commercials all in the same day each week. You could be an advertiser who "owns" Tuesdays on one radio station. You could run eight ads every Tuesday from 6:00 a.m. to 7:00 p.m.

Many, if not most radio stations have sufficient numbers of people in their audience to generate a few prospects per day for almost any business. Once you determine the audience profile and match that with your customer profile, you can determine if a particular station fits your needs.

Here's how: listen to the station and write down the names of five local advertisers who are not your competitors. Call them (at a convenient time) and ask them a few questions. *We wouldn't ask them about the results they get because they may or may not really know. Chances are they don't. But it doesn't matter because you'll be scheduling your ads using a proven formula and not*

according to some concoction brewed up for the convenience of the station.

♦ **Has your station rep served you well?**

♦ **How many different reps have called on you from this station in the past year?**

♦ **Does the station do everything they say they'll do?**

♦ **Are the people at the station arrogant, difficult to work with, as some of the top rated stations are?**

If you like the answers you get, call that station and let them know that you want to buy air time. Do two things:

1. **Give them the schedule you want (not the one they may try to sell you).**

2. **Tell them you'll write your own copy.**

Don't let them talk you out of either.

Direct Mail

The main reason for using direct mail is to promote a purchase or an inquiry.

Direct mail can be very powerful if you target your prospect carefully and if you mail often with some unique offer to get their attention. This is definitely a medium that can pinpoint your prospect and reach that prospect time after time, with great results. This is also a medium that affords a much higher measure of direct accountability than other media.

There are hundreds of direct mailers vying for the attention of your prospect, so repetition and frequency again play a vital role. In fact, your prospect will receive over 100 pieces of direct mail in the same week yours arrives.

Results increase after several mailings, and especially after personal contact, so if you can follow up a mailing with a phone call, all the better.

Don't use direct mail companies that employ a "marriage mailing." A marriage mailing is so called because many different advertisers mail their ads together in one envelope in an attempt to save money. You're almost always better off mailing your own individual piece to your own preferred customers. (If you can justify the dollar return vs. the cost per mailing with a marriage mailing company, fine. We haven't found too many businesses that can make that justification, though there may be some.)

Coupons are bad news! After short-term increases, coupons invariably educate consumers to wait for a lower price, which hurts your growth in the long run. Coupons are seductive, but, in most cases, harmful. Even the large corporations are now seeing that. Many of them are sorry they ever started using coupons.

Some other tips:

- ◆ **Color is effective, and the most effective colors are black and red. If you use black type on white paper with the sparse use of red to highlight or accent, you'll have an attention-getting piece. Other colors can be used as well, and the envelope should be a bright, cheery color.**

◆ Have a big promise on the outside of that brightly colored envelope that compels the recipient to open it.

◆ Don't forget the super headline on the inside! If they don't read that, they won't read anything else.

◆ An envelope that's plain, hand addressed, with no return address is intriguing, and can often get a high rate of return.

◆ People like to see their names in print, so a larger type size for the name of your customer can be attention-getting.

Like other print vehicles, such as newspapers, direct mail is more effective when you are dominating an electronic medium like television, or radio. In this case, name recognition can make a difference. People recognize your name from the electronic media and they pay more attention. They may even have a sense of trust because your name is familiar to them.

Direct mail can be the most efficient means of advertising on a per-sale basis, and it provides a way to compete with any sized local competitor if you follow the direct mail rules. The elements in direct mail to pay absolute attention to are, in order:

1. The list
2. The offer
3. The copy
4. The graphics

We're using the 60-30-10 results ratio here. Sixty percent of your results will depend on the list you use (a preferred customer list is the best). Thirty percent of your results will be determined by the offer you make to the recipient and the copy you write. Ten percent of your results will depend on the aesthetics of the "package."

Another important thing to remember is to mention your mailing campaign in your electronic copy. ("Look for our special offer in this week's mail.") All your copy should work together in that way. Cross-promote the other media for maximum impact. Of course not everyone within ear-shot or eye-shot will receive your mailing piece, but if they're looking for it and they don't find it, they may call and ask you to send one!

Although we cannot recommend that direct mail be used as a primary vehicle for domination for most businesses, it can be very useful as a support vehicle.

Yellow Pages

Like newspapers, the yellow pages is primarily an informational rather than motivational medium. Consumers go to the yellow pages when they need your location or your phone number. They then call you for more information.

Unless you have the biggest and best ad, most of the display ad money you spend in the yellow pages is largely wasted, at least in most business categories.

The yellow pages has better trained salespeople than most media. They'll try to sell you a larger and larger ad every time

you renew, because *upsizing your ad is how most of them make their commissions.*

They're good at what they do, so when they come to turn the screws on you, follow this rule of thumb: *If the greatest percentage of your business is done by customer contact on the phone, have a display ad. If the greatest percentage of your business is conducted at your place of business, have a listing alone.* Or you may be somewhere in between (box ad). Guide yourself according to the number of phone sales you make.

Here are some other yellow pages rules:

◆ **Write your own yellow pages copy.** *The copy is the key!* **Make it an information/sales ad, not a name-address-phone number ad alone. Sell as many of your benefits and features as you have space for.**

◆ **Include your Unique Selling Proposition or Preemptive Advantage.**

◆ **Use a headline as in your newspaper, direct mail, and other print copy.**

◆ **Use the main yellow pages book for your area. Buying ads in every little suburban book is seldom necessary.**

◆ **If you don't run an ad as big or bigger than your competition, you won't be able to compete well in the yellow pages.**

Ask a car dealer with a full page yellow pages ad if he sells any more cars from that ad than a car dealer with a listing alone. If he's

truthful he'll say no, assuming he knows, which is doubtful. Car dealers don't need display ads in the yellow pages, unless a dealer has some very unique service or product, which is unlikely. Other categories can do without display ads in the yellow pages as well. When's the last time you did business with a funeral home because of the size of their yellow pages display ad? Yet some funeral homes waste thousands of dollars a month on full page ads.

Then there's the annual silly season among those business owners who believe that the first yellow pages listing position in their category is a major advantage. Really? Would you trust your fiscal affairs to a company listed as AAA AArdvark Financial Planners, or your mental well-being to the AAA AABBA DABBA Psychiatric Clinic?

This is a true story, though it will sound fabricated. Michael once phoned an auto insurance company listed in the yellow pages under **A AABBOT AH Auto Insurance**, who just happened to have the biggest ad on the page. He jokingly asked the young lady who answered if Mr. AABBOT AH was in and was informed, in what was perceived to be rather testy tones, that their firm's real name was something like Rivers Insurance Company, but that their pseudonym got them "a lot more phone calls." Michael asked how she knew they got more phone calls, and, between audible gum chews, she righteously announced, "it got you to call us, so I guess it worked with you!" When he politely informed her that hers was the ninth company he called and that he had gotten the best quote from an independent agent named Wojtusak, who had a one line listing, she hung up on him!

Touchy clan, those AABBOT AH's.

Are gullible business owners being led by yellow pages salespeople to actually believe that an "A" name will produce more phone calls? If that's true, every business in America whose name doesn't begin with several A's will never get the highly coveted first position in the listings, nor as many phone calls as those with an A position, so they might as well not be in the yellow pages at all! Suggest that logic to your yellow pages salesperson and see how quickly the concept "backpeddle" comes to life.

Don't ever tell people to look for your ad or your phone number in the yellow pages. Tell them to look you up in the white pages. There are no competitors' ads in the white pages.

THE INTERNET

The answers are still out on the use of the Internet as a viable medium for local business owners. The numbers change every day and the information under this heading will no doubt change with subsequent printings. There are some things worth noting though.

This medium may well be to the new century what TV was to the preceding. Our interest here is the impact the Internet has or will have on local commerce, which is far from evident at this point. The feedback is that the Internet has not effected local sales positively for most categories of retail or sevice businesses. There are very few exceptions.

It is entirely possible that the Internet will eventually become a viable force for local business but this is what we refer to as an "intentional" medium, meaning the consumer must intentionally go to the ad, as with newspapers, yellow pages and the like. The

ad in those media does not go to the consumer as it does with "unintentional" media like TV and Radio. The result is that Internet businesses will have to use the unintentional media, Radio and TV, to influence consumers to intentionally visit their Internet site. Many national companies are spending hundreds of millions of dollars on unitentional media for that purpose. Can local businesses afford to do the same, even on a lesser scale? A mention of your web site, if you have one, can be made in your other local advertising, but to buy local air time just to advertise a web site that may or may not have any local viability is an unaffordable venture for most business owners.

National companies and chain stores have universally used the Internet to advertise low price. Most of those same companies are also losing money from their use of the Internet. There may be a connection. There is no greater strength the Internet can offer than convenience. So why are most Internet advertisers giving their profits away? Ask yourself, does your local convenience store compel you to shop there by advertising low prices? Do you shop there on occasion because their milk is cheaper, or because it's closer, handier, time saving? The stores on the Internet may be missing the boat on this one, and their profit pictures seem to bear that out.

This is the classic "reach" versus "frequency" dilemma. We'll opt for the smaller number and greater impact for steady growth until someone proves us wrong. The Internet is a seductive, alluring, still novel medium but until we see signs of consistent growth for a wider range of local businesses, we sug-

gest you marvel at this advertising vehicle from afar, at least for the time being.

To Be Continued.

The Goal

As you can see, each of the mass media has specific strengths and weaknesses relative to domination and impact. Your job is to find the mass media that are most suitable to your budget, and to your objectives of establishing an equity position in a short time, say a few weeks, and of providing the impact necessary to motivate a few new prospects on a daily basis. This is all done by reaching "sufficient" numbers of consumers in your target market. "Sufficiency" is the key.

"Sufficient" numbers are going to vary with each business. A fast food chain needs to reach many times more prospects than our example business, Acme Jewelers. The reason they'll need more reach is that a fast food average ticket is less than one/100th that of our jeweler and it will take many tickets to produce any sizeable growth. Of course a fast food chain has a lot of repeat business, so a new customer for a fast food place may be worth 50 or 100 tickets or more per year, as opposed to Acme's one or two.

Let us give you a general guideline to what we mean by "sufficient": You'll want to reach enough people to motivate the total daily prospect count you'll need, in order to reach your growth objective. Start that process by dominating one member of one medium (e.g., one radio station or one TV program) and grow out from there.

When you advertise at minimum frequency levels week after week, month after month, you're taking what's called the "rifle approach" or "dominating the media."

Depending on your budget, you could dominate several media, or one medium, or one member of one medium. Your budget will also determine your growth objective. The more you have to spend, the higher the growth objective.

Whatever your case may be, keep in mind that almost any member of any medium reaches sufficient numbers of your prospects to motivate a few people a day to come into your business, or phone your business if that's how you operate.

If you reach small numbers of prospects at minimum frequency levels you will quickly establish an equity position with those prospects in a few weeks. This assumes you are an advertiser who can afford to do so. If you cannot afford to buy the kind of impact necessary to gain your equity position in a few weeks time, that doesn't mean you can't begin the process. Begin by determining just where you are now, and where you want to go. The following definitions will help you make those determinations:

There are essentially three levels of advertising:

A level–frequency/consistency/reach
B level–frequency/consistency
C level–consistency

The **A level** advertiser can afford to dominate (frequency) at least one member of one medium, what we'll call the primary vehicle for domination, on an ongoing basis (consistency),

and can afford occasional schedules in support media, or those media use to support the primary medium for domination (sufficient reach).

The **B level** advertiser is one who can afford to dominate at least one member of one medium on a limited basis, such as one TV(frequency) on an ongoing basis (consistency) but who cannot afford a great deal of advertising in support media (limited reach). For this advertiser, a more conservative growth objective should be set.

The **C level** advertiser is one who cannot afford to dominate a primary vehicle for domination (limited frequency) and who cannot afford support media (very limited reach) but who can afford to be advertising in some consistency, like one day each week. If this is you, you're an S.B.N. (Something's Better than Nothing" advertiser. The reason "something's better than nothing" is this: the only guarantee in advertising is, *if you don't schedule any ads at all, no one's going to read them, see them, or hear them.*

Understand The Basics Of Electronic Media Ratings

Frankly, we don't like the subject of ratings very much. A lot of damage has been done to local advertisers as a result of the self-serving misuse of ratings information by some media salespeople. In addition, too many ad agencies use the research to avoid accountability. ("We bought everything by the book. It must have been the weather.")

Because, however, media ratings are a fact of advertising life, it's better to know some definitive information, if only as a defensive measure, than to not know it at all. Ultimately you will need very little information in order to make productive buys in the local electronic media, but because media salespeople are going to continue to try and sell you on favorable research, it's better for you understand what they're really saying than to be at the mercy of their self-serving interpretations.

The television and radio media have research services that provide them with information about the people who listen to or view their programs. Their information or research is commonly called "the ratings," or "the numbers," or "the book." TV and radio stations pay tens of thousands of dollars every year for information they can use to convince you to buy time on their medium. By using the ratings research, media salespeople can show you that a certain program or time slot attracts a certain number of listeners or viewers of a particular age and gender. They also have information about their audiences' income, zip codes, education level, and spending habits.

The salespeople from each electronic medium can use the ratings to match the customer profile of your business with a specific program or time slot.

They show you why it's more cost efficient to buy air time from them than from another electronic competitor. They point out that the competing station or program reaches fewer consumers in your target market, or if the competing station or program reaches more of your target market, it may be at a higher cost per viewer or listener reached. They will then give you the advantage of their stations' "cost per point." (They do not talk about Real Issues like "cost per prospect," which is all that really matters.)

All of the talk and information about the ratings can be extremely confusing because media salespeople have used the ratings to debunk another salesperson's claims, or to bolster their own claims, or both.

It soon becomes apparent that the ratings can easily be manipulated in favor of the seller.

Having stated our concerns about the misuse of the ratings, we think it's important for you to at least have an adequate understanding of what media salespeople are talking about when they use certain terms.

The 33 Ruthless Rules of Local Advertising

116

Definitions – Radio

Cume

The "cume" is the number of unduplicated listeners who tuned into a station for at least five minutes of a particular time period.

Example: Station WXXX has a *cume* audience of 50,000 among Adults 18+, Monday–Sunday, 6 a.m.–Midnight.

Explanation: WXXX has 50,000 unduplicated listeners per week who are over the age of 18, who listened to WXXX for at least 5 minutes between 6:00 a.m. and Midnight, sometime between Monday and Sunday.

Average Quarter Hour Persons

The Average Quarter Hour Persons, are the average number of people in a particular demographic who listen to a station for at least 5 minutes during an average quarter hour within a given time period.

Example: Station WXXX has 5,000 average quarter hour listeners among adults 18-49 years old, Monday-Friday, 6 a.m.–7 p.m.

Explanation: In any given quarter hour between 6:00 a.m. and 7:00 p.m., Monday through Friday, station WXXX has an average of 5,000 listeners who tuned in for at least 5 minutes during any given quarter hour.

Average Quarter Hour Rating

This is the average quarter hour persons audience for a demographic group expressed as a percentage of all persons estimated to be in that demographic group.

Example: Station WXXX has an average quarter hour rating of 5.0 among adults 18–34, 6-10 a.m., Monday–Friday.

Explanation: 5% of all people in the market who are between 18 and 34 are listening to station WXXX during any given quarter hour between 6:00 a.m. and 10:00 a.m. Monday thru Friday.

Net Frequency

The Net Frequency is the average number of times that a listener is exposed to a commercial within the expressed time period.

Example: An advertiser runs a commercial schedule on station WXXX to reach adults, 25-54 listening from 6:00 a.m. to 7:00 p.m., Monday thru Friday, an average of 3 times each.

Explanation: This means that a sufficient number of commercials ran between the time period 6:00 a.m. to 7:00 p.m., Monday thru Friday, to result in the average number of listeners between the ages of 25 and 54 hearing the commercial

an average of 3 times during
that period.

Cost Per Point (CPP)

The Cost Per Point is the cost of each
rating point for a specific schedule.
Determining the cost per point is the current
preferred means of media and ad agencies
to judge the relative competitiveness of a
station's rate card within the market.

Example: Station WXXX tells you they
            are more cost efficient because
            their cost per point is lower.

Explanation: To determine a station's cost
            per point, and thus their rela-
            tive rate efficiency among
            stations, divide the average
            rate per spot by the station's
            average quarter hour rating
            for the time period you're
            buying. If the average rate
            for your schedule is $50 per
            spot, and the station's aver-
            age quarter hour rating for
            the time period is 5.0, your
            cost per point is $10, or $50
            divided by 5.0.

Definitions – Television

Rating

A Rating is the estimated percent of
television households or persons tuned to a
specific station during a specific program.

Example:	The 6 o'clock local news on station KYYY-TV achieves a 10 rating among adults 25-54.
Explanation:	This means that the 6 o'clock news on KYYY- TV is reaching 10 percent of all persons in the market between the ages of 25 and 54 during the measured time period.

Share

The Share is estimated percent of households using television (HUT) or persons using television (PUT) and who are tuned to a specific program or station.

Example:	The 6 o'clock local news on KYYY-TV achieves a 20 share among adults 25-54.
Explanation:	This means that 20 percent of all adults 25 to 54 years old who are watching television during the time period, are watching the 6 O'clock news.

Reach

Reach is the estimated number of unduplicated or different households or persons who watched a specific station at least once for at least 5 minutes during the week in the reported time period.

Example:	The 6 o'clock news on station KYYY-TV reaches 100,000 people per week, ages 25-54.
Explanation:	This means that 100,000 people per week who are between the ages of 25 and 54 tune into the 6 O'clock news on KYYY-

TV for at least 5 minutes during the period measured.

Gross Rating Points

Gross Rating Points are the total number of rating points achieved in a market with a particular schedule of commercials.

Example: Your commercial schedule on KYYY-TV achieves 100 gross rating points.

Explanation: This means that the number of commercials you ran, times the individual rating points of the programs you ran in, equaled 100 gross rating points for the overall commercial schedule.

Two appropriate uses of the ratings research are:

1. **To determine just how many ads you'll have to run to get the minimum frequency levels you want, and to determine the demographic profile of an audience.**

2. **Once you've done your own "seat of the pants" evaluation of the local media, you can then review their research to determine if you're getting the best price you can, all things being equal.**

For instance: If two TV stations want your business and both have the same number of people in your target market viewing their respective programs, buy the one who'll give you the best rate. But if one program has, say,

5,000 viewers at cost of $75 per ad, and another has 7500 viewers at a cost of $100 per ad, buy more commercials for the same money on the less expensive program, even though the more expensive rate looks like a good deal, given the additional viewers.

Why? *Because you'll get more impact with more commercials.*

Greater frequency of message will give you a better chance of motivating more people from the audience of five thousand than the audience of seventy-five hundred by virtue of the number of times you can get your message to them. (This assumes, of course, that you follow the copy Rules.)

Stop Spraying And Praying

Don't worry about the consumers you can't afford to reach!

There is a word that describes people who have succumbed to the popular, alluring, seductive notion that "the more people you reach with your ad, the better chance you have of growing." The word is "scammed."

Local advertisers may buy TV, radio, newspaper, bus benches, and billboards, but not get much impact with any one of them. This is the result of what's called the "shotgun" approach to advertising. It's also called "spraying and praying." This approach delivers large numbers of people, but no consistent impact. Lots of reach, little frequency. Lot's of hope, little returns.

Successful local advertising is not a function of reaching large numbers of people. It is a function of convincing the relatively few prospects you can afford to reach to do business with you, and not your competitors!

In other words, if you're going to worry about anything in local advertising, worry if the people you are reaching with your ads are being reached with enough impact to turn them in your direction.

You cannot expect to compete effectively when you scatter your ad budget to the local media winds. It simply doesn't work, unless you spend far more than you have to, and take many years more than necessary to build your equity position.

Use A Proven Scheduling Formula

Schedule your advertising to give your message the most growth impact it can have:

1. Choose a medium to dominate.

For most local advertisers this should be an electronic vehicle—radio or television. If you have to start small, fine. You can always start with a conservative growth objective and add advertising dollars and media as you grow.

2. Determine if your chosen medium for domination reaches a sufficient number of your target consumer.

Once you've identified your target consumer, and the individual stations that reach your target, almost any one of those stations will have sufficient audience to affect your growth. But if you are the exception, that is a business with a small average ticket and a high floor traffic count (grocery store, convenience store, fast food restaurant), you may have to increase your reach by adding dayparts, programs or media.

3. Schedule your electronic ads for impact.

Schedule your radio ads every week for the first sixteen weeks and three out of every four weeks thereafter. Make sure you get three net impressions per week.

Ask your TV rep for a schedule that gives you 250 gross rating points (GRP's) per two week run. Schedule your TV ads for two weeks out of every month for the entire twelve month period. This TV schedule will result in at least three net impressions during each two-week run.

4. Determine the relative affordability of the schedule.

Can your expected floor traffic increases sustain your advertising efforts? Even if you spend all your initial profits on advertising, if the new customers bring in many times your expenditure in repeat and referral business, your expense is justifiable and relatively affordable. (See Rule 6)

5. Make a twelve-month buy with a four-month option.

It will take three to four months at net frequency levels of three per week to establish an equity position for those businesses who have not had a long or consistent advertising history. The "3 net" frequency levels are also critical because of the need to attract customers or prospects from your competitor's Now Buyer pool.

Tell your media rep you want any discounts that come with a twelve-month schedule, but you also want an option to

cancel after 16 weeks, with no rate penalty, if the results aren't to your satisfaction.

Here's another notion that has little if any basis in fact, assuming you know how to schedule (long term, with impact) your ads: many local advertisers have the false impression that running ads at the end of the week, Thursday, Friday and Saturday, is better than running ads at the beginning of the week. Why?

Is there no one shopping at the beginning of the week?

Do shoppers always wait until Friday or Saturday to make their shopping plans?

Most advertisers think of media as vehicles for short-term results. That's also why they wait until late in the week to advertise their goods/services. If the media are used for their long-term strengths, running ads only near the weekend or, in the case of the electronic media, only in certain time periods, reflects a misunderstanding of how the media and consumers operate. *If you're advertising with a dominant, consistent schedule, it doesn't matter on which days you run your ads!*

So why not run them when there's less competition around you? Let other advertisers compete with each other amidst all the end-of-week ad clutter. You can do your ad scheduling on Sunday, Monday, Tuesday, and Wednesday. And you'll almost certainly get a lower ad rate when you buy ads for the first few days of the week.

The only exceptions might be if you're having a special weekend event and you want to run ads leading right up to the occurrence. Or, if your competition is always in the paper on the same day and in

127

the same section, you should be in the paper with them. The same is not true for the electronic media. People reading the paper may know from habit that ads for certain businesses, like grocery stores, always run on the same day every week. Don't try to change that habit, it will be too expensive.

Also, when you run your newspaper ads, promote them in the electronic media: "look for our ad in this Sunday's Tribune."

Demand Absolute Accountability

Hold your advertising dollars accountable:

1. *Set up a monthly tracking system* that shows you changes from the same month last year in:

    Daily floor traffic count
    Average ticket
    Closing percentage
    Gross sales

    Check also for any changes in repeat and referral business percentages, if possible. This isn't easy to determine, but if you can, it's worth the effort.

2. *As you compare the changes this year* with the same month last year, it is vital to note any local and national economic trends and any internal or external marketing bridge changes that may have occurred. These variables can help explain the results you get.

3. *At the end of four months*, evaluate your advertising results. If, by then, you can see that you've reached the average percentage of growth that you need each month to achieve your growth objective by the end of the 12-month growth objective period, the program is working.

4. *Any copy or scheduling changes* that may have to be made to accelerate the growth process can only be determined by the results of the tracking system you put in place. The tracking system is your key to absolute accountability.

Part FIVE

Protecting Your Progress

Never Get Diverted From The Real Issues

Would you rather spend $100 on an ad that produced $120 in net profits, or $1 on an ad that returned nothing?

You wouldn't think that was a silly question with the emphasis that's placed on low rates and cost efficiency by media salespeople and local advertisers. Some advertisers boast about their low media rates, and some media reps laugh about how they got you anyway, but that whole subject may be just another diversion, another red herring that keeps everyone distracted while the Real Issues get lost in the confusion.

If you're not focused on the Real Issues, you'll never know if you're winning efficiently, no matter what your rates are!

Here's what discussions with your media reps and ad agencies should be about:

◆ **Are my gross sales satisfactory?**

◆ **Is my advertising producing consistent results?**

◆ **Is there growth available for me in the marketplace?**

◆ **Can I justify my ad budget amount?**

- Can I identify and correct anything in my marketing bridge that's getting in the way of my complete advertising success?

- Is there a formula that can help me write dynamic copy?

- Is there a way to set a measurable growth objective for my ad budget?

- Is there a specific way to use the media to gain an equity position and measurable growth?

- Is there a simple system of absolute accountability that allows me to determine the effectiveness of my ad expenditures?

Don't Forget How People Remember

People make decisions to purchase goods and services in the subconscious mind. The easiest way to get through the conscious mind and into the subconscious mind is by repetition. The objective is to inform, persuade, and *remind*. Remind people in a way that generates consistent growth as you inform and persuade them.

How did we learn to ride a bicycle, walk, read, and remember your phone number? We all learned the same way, and that is by repetition. *Repetition is the key to learning anything.*

Remember, people forget. You have to remind them constantly of your Name, Location, Unique Selling Proposition, or Preemptive Advantage constantly. If you don't, they'll forget.

A successful advertising endeavor includes Informing, Persuading, and Reminding.

Remember, you're not advertising to a standing army—it's a passing parade.

You must constantly remind the passing parade.

(Just a reminder.)

Sell Something More Profitable Than Low Price

Out of one hundred prospects, how many will not do business with you because of price? If you are the kind of business that's positioned themselves as a discount house and you don't have the discounts, you'll probably lose a fairly large percentage of prospects to a lower price. But what if you're not positioned as a major price discounter? Out of one hundred prospects, you'll lose only nine prospects to a lower price. And if you are known for your excellent service, you'll retain ninety-one out of a hundred customers.

We know of a delicatessen with prices twenty to thirty percent higher than a nearby competitor, and a lot higher than the next door grocery, which carries some of the same lines as this deli. But the deli's business continues to grow. How? By giving their customers incredible, personal service, by remembering their customers' names and by being maniacal about quality.

They also advertise the fact that they give their customers what they really want. They tell consumers how good their products are, in detail, and what that means to the consumer. They have established themselves as the place to go if you want the very best.

The deli put together a brochure that presents a particular cheese product in a very knowledgeable, interesting way. The brochure has key words like "discovering" (32 different cheeses...), "how to," "free," and so forth. The brochure presents the product in a way that has the reader think of that deli as experts, as the authorities on cheeses. It asks, "Why go elsewhere?"

The brochure doesn't just "talk" to the reader about cheese. It also gives the reader an easy way to become their own cheese and wine experts. The deli discovered that a powerful factor for people buying specialty cheeses or wines was to impress others. A customer get wine or cheese, and they get a way to impress guests at their next dinner party. Talk about finding a USP/PA.

One thing this wildly successful business never does is advertise a low price. They found something far more attractive to sell.

Avoid The "Sale" Syndrome

Sales can be useful if used sparingly. Consumers are assaulted by so called "sales" every day. Advertisers use any excuse to have a sale. Consumers have become disbelieving as a result of retailers who will use any excuse to have a sale. As a result, the only sales that are viewed as legitimate are those conducted by companies that have very few of them.

If you're overstocked and have a cash flow problem, one tendency is to get into the "sale" habit. Companies who constantly rely on sales to save them soon find they've fallen into a costly trap. Not only are there better ways to move inventory, but *you have to put in twice the effort just to be where you were!*

For example: Let's say you mark up your items 50% above cost. You mark up an item that cost you $10 to $15, so you have a $5 gross profit. On ten sales you'd gross $50 at this original price. Now you have a sale. Your $15 items are discounted 15%. The sale price becomes $12.75. You now have a gross profit of $2.75. To get gross profits approaching $50 you'd have to sell eighteen units! ($2.75 x 18 sales = $49.50.) *Nearly 80% more unit sales for about the same profits!*

Advertisers will say that they have no choice but to compete on price. Of course there's a choice. If price were the primary buying criteria in the consumer community, how could convenience stores stay open? You can drop a paycheck in a convenience store! They stay open because they have a Unique Selling Proposition/Preemptive Advantage called convenience! People will pay for convenience. They'll also pay for service, and quality, and many other benefits you can turn into USP's and PA's.

It's true that some businesses and even some categories of businesses are known for being more price competitive than others. That's the hole they've dug themselves into. But remember, for most categories, only about 9 percent of sales are lost due to price.

If you think sales will be a way to gain regular customers, think again. *The people who are really price conscious will go to whoever has the lowest price.*

You'll never get all of the market, so why try to get it all by slashing your margins so thin that you finally have to close your doors (after your final sale!)?

In a few cases a business can be perceived as a low-priced operator while maintaining a decent per-item profit. If you're one of those, keep up the good work for as long as you can.

Often a business will have a "sale" or advertise a sale price in reaction to what their competitors are advertising. You could be following the competitors right into a black hole. Your problems and opportunities are not necessarily the same or anywhere near those of your competitors. So, just do what you do well and let them do what they do.

You're either making dust or eating dust. Stop eating your competitor's dust. It could be polluted.

Let Your Employees In On Your Advertising Plans

Strange as it may seem, few companies let their own employees know what the company is advertising!

We've called businesses several times with a question about an advertised item only to be told by an employee that they aren't familiar with the ad or the offer!

Let everyone in the company know about your advertising plans. Have meetings. Read them your copy. Tell them where you're advertising, when, and for what purpose. Show new employees your yellow pages ad and explain it. Show them your advertising scrapbook and explain the companies' advertising philosophy. Make them aware of the importance of knowing the what's, when's and where's of your advertising.

If you can excite your employees with your advertising plans and ads, your employees can then excite the prospects that your advertising is bringing in or causing to telephone.

Let Go
Of The Branch

A man was walking along the bank of a raging river. He suddenly stumbled into the water and grabbed a slippery tree branch that was hanging over the side of the bank. He couldn't pull himself toward the river bank because of the force of the current working against him. Over and over the man yelled loudly for help.

After a seemingly endless period, a lone, powerful voice said, "I can help you." Our desperate friend was delighted to hear a voice answer his cries for help, though he could see no one. The voice said, "If you want me to save you, you'll have to trust me and do exactly as I say." "I'll do anything you say," said our friend. "Good," came the reply, and then the slowly but firmly spoken words, "let go of the branch and I'll save you."

The desperate man gave some very critical, very agonizing thought to this demand. In a few seconds he looked up toward the unreachable river bank and hollered loudly, "Is there anybody else around who can help me?"

There wasn't.

Often our traditions, beliefs, opinions, preferences, circumstances, and rules get challenged. For the most part, people choose to remain well inside their comfort zones.

They resist having to choose something they aren't familiar with or don't have experience with, even if it means taking a bigger chance by not doing so. And so it is with a new advertising approach. You may have to let go of your own "branch" before putting what we've outlined so far into action.

If, as We've stated before, more than ninety percent of local business owners are disappointed with the results they get from their advertising, why do they continue writing or approving tired, ineffectual copy and buying arbitrary, impotent media schedules?

That kind of behavior reminds us of contemporary novelist Rita Mae Brown's definition of "crazy." "Crazy," she says, "is doing the same thing over and over while expecting a different result."

Common Sense
Marketing

Keeping In
Mind
Mark Twain's
Observation
That
"Common
Sense Ain't
All That
Common"

Find Low-cost Services You Can Perform Better Than Your Competitors

As a local advertiser, trend or pace setting requires extremely careful media scheduling and extraordinary ad copy. But what if you're not an advertiser? What if you haven't reached the level where advertising is affordable to you? You can still be a pacesetter among your competitors.

You can dominate a segment of the market more effectively than your largest competitor, and doing so may not cost as much or be as difficult to accomplish as you first think. For instance, setting the pace for a business your size might mean nothing more than being more diligent than your competitors when it comes to calling your customers by phone and asking them if their buying experience went well. If your competitors don't do that or don't do it as memorably (formulate a creative conversation) as you, you set and control the pace, the trend, and the advantage in demonstrating customer concern.

Ask Five Key People
For Five Referrals
Each

Someone once said, "there's no shortage of contributors in the world, just a shortage of contributees." People are waiting to be asked to give something that they're willing to give, but it seems there is a shortage of people willing to take the gift.

People really want to contribute. For the most part, all that's needed is the asking. Ask for referrals. You may be surprised.

Know and Articulate Three Basic Messages About You And Your Business

When someone asks what you do, add something intriguing to your answer besides your profession or the name of your business. Instead of saying "I'm in the restaurant business, say, "I'm John Smith, and I serve food to some of the finest diners in the city." Or, "I'm a restaurateur who believes that his dining guests are the most important people on earth." Or, "I own (or work in) a business where every customer has to be happier walking out than when they walked in."

That kind of response will undoubtedly elicit interest, especially if you're speaking to a potential customer.

Immediately Acknowledge A Referral

Let very little water pass under the marketing bridge before you acknowledge the person responsible for making the referral. This is more than good business, it's more than smart business; it's critical business.

Never be too busy to thank, acknowledge, or recognize satisfied customers who are talking about you and thus serving as outside salespeople for your business.

Become A Known Resource To Your Customers

Get to know intimately two-dozen highly qualified people who, though not in your field, could provide various services that your ideal clientele may need. Then make referrals to your clientele. We doubt that your competitors do this as a matter of course.

Become the person your customers trust to steer them to the people and businesses who can help them with their needs.

You might know a good accountant, a good mechanic, a good clothier, banker, attorney or dry cleaner. If you know these sources to be very reliable, trustworthy, and honest, share them with your ideal clientele.

Of course, if you can't verify your sources, don't make a recommendation.

Become Known As Unconditionally Honest

This suggestion requires some unselfishness on your part. Let people know how they can get what they want, even if it occasionally means you don't get their business. There's a strong chance that those people who benefited by your constructive suggestions and referrals might tell others who can use your services.

Put another way, never exploit the prospect. Always go out of your way to help them. There's a payback down the road somewhere even if you don't see it immediately.

Share Your Vision

What are you committed to? What's your personal and professional vision? What gets you on your feet and going day after day?

Once you have a vision and can share it with others, you may find that other people share your vision or are at least willing to support you in realizing yours. But you have to be able to share your vision in a way that enlists others, interests them, intrigues them. People are often enlisted in someone else's vision just because of the level of enthusiasm with which the vision is communicated. People like being around lively, vital, and energetic entrepreneurs. That kind of vitality can be contagious. Everything we accomplish in our lives has occurred because of the support and contribution of others.

Make A Referral Tree

The life or death of many businesses depends on the referrals they get, or don't get. List your ten best referral sources and then work that list.

Don't be shy about this. Most people will come around, given an opportunity to help, so give them that opportunity.

Once you get good new referral sources, put them on your list as well.

Tell People What You Want For Them

Instead of telling people what you want for yourself (I'd like to make a lot of money), try telling them what you want for them. Do you want them to experience complete satisfaction from having done business with you? Would you like them to gain personal success? What do you want for them?

Answer that question in one phrase, communicate it to your employees, then deliver it, and you're on your way to having a very prosperous entity.

One businessman we worked with told us that he sincerely wanted every one of his customers to "feel like they had won" after doing business with him. His employees were trained to want the same thing. His was an industry replete with credibility problems. A 25% repeat business ratio was very good. His repeat business was close to 65%!

The customers of this business evidently not only felt they had won, they told others as well. The referral business percentages increased dramatically as well. And all that happened out of a commitment to generate a feeling in his customers, the feeling that comes with having "won" by doing business with him.

Know What You Cannot Or Will Not Offer

This is also called the "no surprises" suggestion. Be clear about what you can give, but be clearer still about your limits.

Sometimes a business owner or an employee can get carried away with promises to a prospective customer. What's been promised can't be delivered. It's better to give a prospect away to a competitor than to have them speaking ill of you.

Know Exactly What Your Strengths Are, And Then Let Others Know Them

Don't over promise. Don't under deliver. Determine what you can do for others and then do that every time. Let people know what you're good at and what they can count on from you.

Repeat and referral business is a by-product of consistently demonstrating your strengths. If you're a legal or medical or financial professional, your strengths could be your manner or your trustworthiness, or the fact that you give others peace of mind. If you're a plumber, your strength could be your follow-up personal check to guarantee your customer's satisfaction. Or you might offer a unique guarantee. Here's the "strengths" marketing plan:

1. Identify or create specific, needed strengths in your business.

2. Market your strengths.

3. Demonstrate your strengths by fulfilling them.

4. Get customer testimonials for your strengths.

5. Hone, polish and "strengthen" your strengths.

Make Your Customers Right (Because They Are)

If you stood in your customers' shoes, saw what they saw, experienced what they experienced and perceived what they perceived, you could not help but understand a complaint.

Maybe from your perspective they aren't right, but don't act that way. The trick is to make them right about their perceptions, whether you agree or not. This suggestion also works in personal relationships—but that's another book.

Personally Survey (Poll) Your Customers

Work the cash register or the equivalent at your business for a few hours each week. Ask your customers what pleased and didn't please them when doing business with you. Tell them you'd be very grateful if they'd be honest with you about their perceptions and experiences.

Find out just how your customer feels after an encounter with your business. The way a customer feels is going to determine repeat and referral business. If your customer doesn't feel comfortable, happy, or enthusiastic about doing business with you, find out why.

Think of your customers as being in charge of your success. If they know you're sincere about wanting suggestions and observations, you can count on them to tell you things you'll never hear from your employees or managers. You don't necessarily have to agree or disagree with the customer's perceptions, just listen carefully.

After gathering the data, act strongly and decisively on any negative items.

Handle Complaints Immediately And Thoroughly

Here's the bad news on complaints: Out of 100 people who are upset with something in your business, 96 of them will never tell you. Instead they'll tell an average of 18 other people! And then 90 of the 96 will take their business to a competitor, unless you immediately and thoroughly handle the complaint. If you really handle the complaint, 95 of 100 customers who had the complaint will return to do business with you.

Who's handling the complaints of your customers? Are they doing it immediately and thoroughly?

Become A Master At Converting Leads Into Customers

What does it cost you to let a prospective customer slip through your fingers?

The first cost is the money you spent bringing the customer in or getting them to call. Then you've lost the profit on the initial sale you failed to make. You then lost all of the repeat business you might have had, as well as any referral business.

Get trained. Do whatever it takes to be good at converting leads. You're in business to generate prospects so that you can make those prospects customers.

If your salespeople haven't mastered turning a prospect into a buyer, get them trained as well. No amount of advertising or marketing can replace a "conversion expert." Every time you lose an un-converted prospect to a competitor, you increase your lead or prospect costs.

Whatever your conversion percentage is now, set a goal to increase it by another increment immediately. If you're selling one out of ten now, up that to two out of ten. If you're selling nine out of ten now, up that to 9.2 out of ten.

Get Your
Personal Needs
Met From
Your Business

Each of us has personal needs that, when met, produce enjoyment, fulfillment, satisfaction.

If you have a need to be recognized, respected, appreciated, organized, successful, or secure, why not have your business be the place where those needs get fulfilled? What are our efforts in the work place all about, if not fulfilling our personal needs?

Think about it.

Treat Your Telephone Like A Profit Center

Inexplicably, many business owners don't conduct phone training.

There are countless cases in every type of business where bona fide prospects were turned into annoyed former prospects because of the way they were handled on the phone.

Customers want to communicate with good listeners, and when you make communication difficult for them, they'll find someone else to do business with.

Whoever answers your phone is really **you**. Whatever perception they get as a result of their phone call to your business will be of you, your business, your professionalism and your credibility.

If you can't train the person(s) answering your phone to behave as though you were taking the call, get rid of them. They'll hurt you repeatedly, though you won't even know it. If you don't know how much money your phone receptionist or the equivalent at your business makes or loses for your business from month to month, you ought to find out.

Unless you're a captain of industry with 5,000 employees, *stop screening your phone calls*. Screening your calls in some cases is understandable and even necessary, but not for a "small," local business.

We've heard all of the reasonable explanations why you must not be interrupted when working. After all you're a very busy person and you have highly legitimate reasons why your calls must be screened. That's one way to view this seemingly inconsequential matter. Here's another:

Michael has a friend in Palm Beach worth more than $100 million for whom he's done some work. As the owner of several small businesses and considerable property, he is a very busy person. But if you were a customer of his and you wanted to get him on the phone to, say, register a complaint, you'd only have to dial the number of his office and ask for him.

When asked why an important, busy man like him didn't screen his calls. He looked at Michael and explained deliberately and clearly—as though speaking to a slow child—that anyone who expected to amount to anything would want to know every detail about how his employees were handling his business. He said that one sure way to know what's working and what's not is to talk directly to customers. He spent several hours a week asking his customers questions about their perception of his business, and he never allowed a customer to get the idea that he was too big or too busy to speak with. "In other words," he said, "if you want to talk to me, call me. If my switchboard operator asks who's calling, tell her it's none of her business. Of course she wouldn't ask because she knows better than to get between me and my customers."

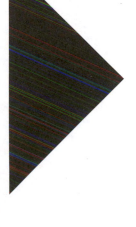

Interesting attitude, and that from a man whom you'd expect would be aloof and difficult to contact. We've never forgotten that conversation. If you must screen your phone calls for whatever reason, make sure your screener does it in a way that does not irritate the caller.

When the caller asks "is ___ in?," don't ask "who's calling" first. Instead, tell the caller whether ___ is in or not, and only then ask who's calling. At least that way callers won't be made to feel like they have no chance for personal contact with the boss.

Here are the questions that cheese-off callers:

◆ **"What is this call in reference to?"**

◆ **"Who may I say is calling?"**

◆ **"What company are you with?"**

◆ **"Will he/she know who you are?"**

◆ **"Does he/she know what this call is about?"**

◆ **"Is he/she expecting your call?"**

Any of those familiar to you?

To Be Interesting, Be Interested

The most interesting people are the most interested people

If you want to be interesting, be interested. Think about it. People want to be listened to, appreciated, heard, paid attention to. They want to know that what they have to say is important to someone else, like yourself.

Being truly interested in other people will distinguish you. It will, in short, make you interesting, and that can make people want to do business with you.

Acknowledge Someone In Person Or In Writing Every Day

People like being noticed when they're contributing. As it says in *The One Minute Manager*, "catch people doing something right."

We suspect that people love to be acknowledged so much because it's so rare.

We're not talking here about complimenting people. One way to differentiate between a compliment and an acknowledgment is this: a compliment normally has something to do with the outside of a person, an acknowledgment with the inside. You may like the way a person dresses and offer a compliment, but if you tell a person that they make a difference just by the way they treat your customers, the way they support your goals, or the supportive attitude they have, that's an acknowledgment.

"I like your shoes," is not an acknowledgment, but "you make a difference to our company and we appreciate your attitude," is.

Establish A Value On Your Time

Find out where your most productive time is spent and spend most of it there. **Stop** spending time doing things that interrupt your **productivity.**

(Like the extra time it took to design this page.)

Have a Company Purpose And Operate By It

If you were to ask a business owner what his/her company purpose was, you would most likely be told it was something about making money or being successful or growing. Company purposes are nearly always profit oriented.

Everyone's for making money and growing a business. That's what this book is all about. But if you think your customers care whether you make money or grow your business or buy a new car or get a new house or retire rich, you are not being realistic. We don't know many customers who would become motivated to spend their money with you because the sign on your door said, "Our purpose is to make more money."

If you were to ask your employees, partners, or accountants what your company purpose was, would you get the same answer from all of them? If not, you're missing out on a fundamental necessity for growing a business.

The reason for having a company purpose is for you and your employees to have a behavior anchor or code in all circumstances, and for your customers to have a public statement of your commitment.

Once you've chosen a company purpose, you have to get agreement for it
from everyone involved with your business, and then you and they have to learn
it, inhale it, absorb it, live it, instill it in
others, manage others from it, and share it
with your customers. Have your company
purpose posted somewhere. Print it on
your pay checks. Bring it up at every staff
meeting. When you expose yourself and
your employees to it enough, it will eventually become second nature.

A company purpose can be very simple or very lengthy. We recommend something simple and memorable like, "Our
purpose is to make sure that every single
customer who walks out of our doors
walks out happier than when they walked
in," or some variation on the service
theme.

Create a company purpose
starting now, and don't let
anything sway you
from carrying it
out. This is not just a
cliché or a trite phrase we're talking about, it's the strength, health, and
vitality of your business that's at stake. If
you and the people around you don't have
a company purpose, you're at the mercy of
everybody's "best intentions."

Are you prepared to bet your business
on someone else's "best intentions?"

Emerson said, "I speak not so much to be understood, but so as not to be misunderstood."

The way to know how effective we are at communicating is by the results we achieve. If we aren't happy with the results, we can ask ourselves, "what could I have said or done that might have produced a better outcome?"

It will take some courage to be open to the answers, and even more courage to implement the corrections, but the results may well be worth the discomfort of taking full responsibility for effective communication.

Here's a worthy challenge: practice your communication skills at home, among your family. There's no place like home to see how well you're doing with communication skills. If you can communicate successfully at home, you can communicate successfully anywhere!

Tell People What You Want Them To Do

If you don't tell people what you want from them, there's a good chance you won't get it. Have you ever thought, "If my employees (partners, etc.) really cared, they'd know what I wanted them to do without having to tell them. Or they'd find out on their own."

Not very likely.

Use A Written Agreement In All Cases

Arguments, upsets, breakdowns, and lost profits occur because of ineffective communication.

Our policy is to have all business agreements in writing, and to discuss each detail in the agreement with each signatory. That's the only way to have a clear understanding about what's agreed upon by each party.

We're not saying that written agreements will end all communication problems, but they will resolve them sooner and reduce their frequency.

Think Holistic –
Act Specific

Once you have a company purpose or goal, and you can see the bigger picture, you will almost automatically take the specific actions that further that purpose or goal. Your efforts will be single actions that affect the whole. The future of your business is a product of each single decision, each single action.

Think holistic:
"I'd like to have six locations."

Act specific:
"I'm going to set up an internal customer satisfaction poll this week."

Each specific act serves to further the holistic vision.

Write a Book Or An Article That Challenges Your Profession's Rules

Herb Cohn, in his book, *You Can Negotiate Anything*, says, "We don't see things the way they are, we see things the way we are." We live in a culture that largely believes that things are what they appear to be. We seem to be wired up that way as human beings. Once someone challenges a notion which appears to be reasonable, that challenge gets attention.

We have a friend, Dr. Bob Schwartz, whose best-selling book, *Diets Don't Work*, challenged the entire diet industry. Dr. Schwartz contends that no matter what we've come to accept as the "rules" for dieting, those rules simply don't work. The challenge that diets don't work was issued over a decade ago and has now itself become the rule! Credible diet experts now all agree that diets don't work.

There are scores of out-dated rules and beliefs that are still held sacred by most industries. We'd bet a month's rent on Windsor castle that most members of your industry follow those same anachronistic rules and beliefs. Just as we've found scores of rules to challenge in the advertising and media industries, there are challenges to be made in your industry. Why not write about them? Why not become the debunker noted for his/her foresight?

The geniuses in any industry are almost always contrarians.

Offer To Help Three People Who Are In Trouble, And Can't Afford Your Services

Once again, when you deliver more than is expected of you, you'll have customers who'll become salespeople.

But offering help to the needy gets you even more than that; it allows you to feel good about yourself as a human being. Most of us have evidence for the truth of the saying, "what goes around comes around." We think you'll find that there's a certain powerful force that brings back into your life whatever you put into the lives of others, and putting a little unselfish support into a few lives will pay off many times over.

◆ **If you're an attorney you might volunteer some time at legal aid.**

◆ **A restaurant owner could give away a few meals each week to a big brothers or big sisters organization.**

◆ **A jewelry store could put together inexpensive costume jewelry packets for nursing home patients during the holidays.**

◆ **A florist could donate some flowers or plants to a veteran's hospital.**

Advance
Your Profession

The unsuitable actions of some members of a profession do harm to their profession as a whole. We'll listen to or tell a good lawyer joke like anyone else, but in reality we view our attorneys as professional, fair, and extremely competent.

What would it take today to strengthen the image of your profession? How about operating with total integrity in each circumstance?

Become An Expert Or A "Personality" In Your Field

Enviable increases in business can occur if you can position yourself as an expert, as the local source for information in your field.

The first step is doing some homework. Read all there is to read about the trends, developments and forecasts in your field. Once you've done your research, write or have someone ghost-write a book on your subject. You can self-publish inexpensively and provide free copies to book stores and other outlets. Let them keep all the profits. Your objective is to get your book showcased and to get yourself some exposure.

Become known as a figure of authority and as a local person-ality through public speaking. Make yourself available for discussion groups, fraternal groups, commu-nity groups, civic groups, and church groups. Let these organizations know by phone or mail who you are, what you do, when you're available, and what benefit you can offer the group by speaking to them.

Work on your speech until you have a clear, crisp, interesting, solid talk of no more than 20 minutes duration. Some ancillary methods for exposure and credi-bility might include teaming up with oth-ers in complementary fields to produce information seminars at no or low cost to the participants. For example: An accountant teams up with an attorney, a financial planner, and a management consultant to offer seminars on how local entrepreneurs can guard against losses

and increase their profits in any economic climate.

Or go out on your own:

◆ **A Chiropractor specializes in food allergies and holds seminars for small groups of concerned patient-prospects.**

◆ **An attorney creates a "how to" series (e.g., How to Protect Yourself from Lawsuits) and speaks about it to groups in need of that particular specialty.**

◆ **Buy inexpensive weekend radio time from a small "talk" station. You'll have a 30- minute show that answers queries about your field of expertise and you'll become a recognized expert. Or you could call radio or TV "talk" program producers and offer yourself as an expert guest.**

◆ **Have your name in the title of your business. That personalizes your business and gives you a higher profile. "Mack Brown and Associates" ties you to the consumer's memory better then "City Financial Planning, Inc..."**

◆ **Host regular breakfast or luncheon meetings at your place of business or in a local restaurant and give short** talks on your area of expertise. Start a telephone "hotline" service. Give the callers free information and tell them to call your office number and ask for additional information. When they call, turn then into a customer.

♦ Start a "900" number service. Give advice to people who call. The caller pays a certain amount per minute, which is billed to their phone number, and the phone company sends you your cut after costs. It's inexpensive to start and your service can grow into an additional source of income.

♦ Write "how to" pamphlets or booklets for your customers and prospects. The more you educate your prospects, the more chance you have of being an expert to whom they turn.

♦ Join clubs/organi-zations/charities where your key customers are likely to be members, but this idea comes with a caveat; you can't constantly talk busi-ness with people who are trying to relax and get away from the "shop." Sales dis-cussions have to be of mutual interest.

Do Everything You Say You'll Do...
And A Little Bit More

When you say you'll do something, do it—all of it. When you sell a product or service, live up to every promise or implied promise. Don't close the file until the work is completely finished.

If you really want to be remembered and talked about by your customers, add just a little extra to what you agreed upon.

Package Your Printed Materials To Get Rave Reviews

Advertisements, brochures, office handouts, introduction pieces, and presentation packets are for people you're asking to trust you, your business, and your referrals.

Is your ability to deliver what you promise reflected in the materials seen by prospective customers? Prospective customers know cheap and tacky materials when they see them. They also know stunning and professional materials.

With the different types of inexpensive computer software available now, it's almost criminal to represent yourself with anything other than great looking materials.

In lieu of doing your materials yourself, hire a graphic artist to create them for you. It will be an investment worth many times what you paid.

Send Birthday And Holiday Cards

When you send a card to a loved one, it's usually received as a thoughtful, generous gesture and a sign of your caring and interest. Customers also appreciate receiving an appropriate card on a special occasion. The trick is to not have it look like a technique or a marketing gimmick, like so many cards do.

Incidentally, anything hand written is preferable to those preprinted "Thank You" cards.

Set Your Standards High And Honor Them

Anyone can go into business. The fact that most businesses go out of business within the first two years proves that. The people who survive, prosper, and grow usually have high standards. Sometimes these standards are not even written or conscious but are still followed naturally and unfailingly.

What standards have you formulated and followed?

Determine how you want to be perceived by others. Writing down the standards that, if followed, would create an ideal public perception of you and your business.

Some examples of standards:

◆ A business owner might have a standard for hiring: "I only hire people who believe or advocate my products/services."

◆ One standard for an interior designer might be: "I only take on jobs that interest and excite me."

◆ A dress shop owner's standard for inventory might be: "I will only carry merchandise I'd be proud to wear myself."

Invite
Key People Out
Socially

We're not talking about a once-year-ly company picnic or a holiday office party. We are talking about having people to dinner or another social event. If you can't afford meals, try meeting socially at cost free functions, such as a free outdoor concert or an amateur sports event.

But just who are these "key people?" We consider a key person to be anyone whose input or output effects the profits of your business. You know who they are. Try to find a way to get them into a social circumstance.

Use Sampling As A Sales Tool

If you have a product or a service you can give away free, you'll find this a very lucrative way to market your business. We're sure you've noticed the people in grocery stores who give away food samples. They do that because it introduces people to a product in an inexpensive way, and a lot of that product gets sold as a result.

Another way to apply sampling is to offer a product or service on a trial basis. Many products and services have been sold after people have been given the opportunity to use the product or service for a short period of time, at no cost. In fact, business owners who use this method say that ninety percent or more of all trial basis offers end up as sales.

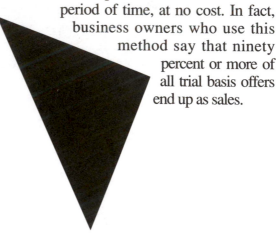

Give Your Product Or Service Away To Three People Who Can Influence Your Business

If you know three people who can be helpful in creating new business for you, give them something that makes it worth their while to do so. You may want to provide them with a service or a product that says "I'm willing to show you that I'm serious about putting your influence to work for me."

It doesn't have to be a costly item, but it should be something that gets their attention and motivates them to action on your behalf.

Deliver More Than Your Customer Is Likely To Expect

When you deliver more than is expected, you exceed the norm, which is usually to offer as little service or as little attention as possible. Do better then the norm, which is not too difficult to do, and you'll have lots of salespeople working for you in the guise of delighted customers.

It doesn't take much to have scores of customers suddenly begin acting as salespeople, simply because a little act makes a big impression.

Send Out
A Newsletter

A personalized newsletter can be educational, informational, interesting, entertaining, and timely. If it's all those things, it's going to get read and you're going to get a net return worth many times whatever time and effort it takes to compile, edit, and mail it.

Your newsletter does not have to be lengthy or complicated. It can be a one page "information" piece that gives some interesting facts about your profession, products, or services.

Send it out quarterly. It's another low cost way to maintain critical customer contact.

Invest In Coaching

A relatively new technology, "Coaching" is, as the word implies, a way to dramatically improve someone's performance.

A business coach is no different from a sports coach in that a business coach observes you and your work and then speaks and listens in a trained way that helps you reach your goals.

Coaching has synthesized the best from such disciplines as psychology, business, and philosophy.

A coach plays several roles. He or she is a Partner who stands by you in tough times. She or he is a Trainer who can show you how to live better and do better, and how to increase personal, communication, and business skills as you work together on reaching your goals. A coach provides you with a structure to excel and to put balance into your life.

A coach will help you:

- ◆ **design your goals**
- ◆ **develop a specific plan of action**
- ◆ **get you in touch with what you really want**
- ◆ **work with and through others to achieve their goals**
- ◆ **remove obstacles**
- ◆ **get your needs met**
- ◆ **balance your personal and business lives**
- ◆ **recover from a major setback or problem**
- ◆ **create a vision that gives you purpose**
- ◆ **set much higher personal standards to live by**
- ◆ **communicate straightforward and fully**
- ◆ **discover hidden, insidious problems**
- ◆ **get you on a rewarding path of personal development**
- ◆ **handle money problems and start saving**
- ◆ **clean up every aspect of your life**

Coaches usually work with their clients by phone. In fact, most coaches and clients never meet, and they work with everyone from bar association presidents, to major corporations, to small business owners.

Coaches usually are surprisingly reasonable when it comes to fees, and getting a good one can change your life.

Under-Promise, But Not Enough To Lose Business

Customers get upset when they have expectations that aren't met by the people they do business with. The expectation is often the result of our communication. We set the customer up to expect more than what is actually delivered.

You're far better off delivering more than your customer expects than to over promise and not deliver. How do you tone down your offer and still get business? The trick is to be realistic, yet motivating. You have to offer your goods or services in a way that's believable and credible, while simultaneously producing a high state of interest. This is a delicate balance that takes some practice, but underselling is a stronger technique than over promising.

Back up your promises and meet your customers' expectations.

Immediately Find Five Ways To Make It Easier For People To Do Business With You

Look at every aspect of your business and ask yourself, "If I were a customer of mine, what would make it easier, or more convenient to do business with me?"

Next, create a list of five strategies that would result in making it easier for people to do business with you. Then follow through on the strategies.

Repeat this exercise every 90 days.

We consider this to be among the most important of any marketing suggestions ever written, by anybody, at any time.

Don't Be A Stranger To Your Customer Base

Regular contact with your customers will increase your sales by a wide margin. If you build a relationship of trust and honesty, you'll have a customer base with which to re-sell, up-sell, and cross-sell. Otherwise growth becomes a game of constantly finding new customers, which is expensive and, at times, almost impossible.

Some suggestions:

◆ **Don't wait for your existing customers to return to you,** *go to them.*

◆ **How often you make contact with a customer depends largely on your product or service. If you sell cars you might want to send a letter once or twice a year. If you sell a product or service that requires a more frequent purchase, make your customer contacts more frequent.**

◆ **Whenever a customer makes a purchase, make a follow-up phone call to them. Let them know how you appreciate their business. Ask if there is anything they have a question about or can be helped with. Tell them to call you personally if they have any problems.**

34

◆ Write personalized letters. Again, find out how things are going with their purchase. Let them know you care. Let them know their value. Let them know you take a personal interest in their satisfaction. Make them feel special.

◆ Offer preferential treatment. Make sure that your existing customer base always gets the best prices, deals, and guarantees you can afford to give.

◆ Give your existing customers a chance to get in on special sale prices before the general public comes in.

Whatever the reason, **Stay in touch with your customers!**

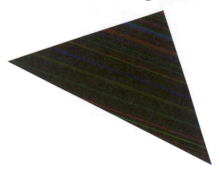

Take A Vacation
Each Quarter

A vacation doesn't have to be a vacation in the traditional sense. It can be a one or two day trip away from your work. Just enough to temporarily rest the machinery.

If you and your spouse, or significant other, can't get away overnight for long stretches, try a 30 or 60 minute drive to another town and have dinner in a restaurant you've never been to. The surroundings will be unfamiliar, the people will be strangers, and you can imagine you are as far away from your daily work routine as you want to be. The "vacation" may last only an hour or two, but it will be refreshing and recuperative. It's only a mini-vacation to be sure, but it really helps.

Take The Initiative - Don't Wait

The best time to act is before the opportunity presents itself. If you have the choice to lead, follow, or get out of the way, we recommend you lead. Better to have followers, than to be one.

A good place to start would be to ask yourself, "In my field, what is wanted or needed?"

When you start getting answers, take the lead in filling the wants and needs.

Do Even More Of The Six Things You Can't Do Too Much Of

1. You cannot service too much.

2. You cannot educate enough.

3. You cannot inform too much.

4. You cannot take follow-up or follow-through too far.

5. You cannot make doing business with you too easy.

6. You cannot make calling or coming into your business too desirable.

THIS WAY TO THE GREAT EGRESS

About The Author

Michael Corbett is arguably America's foremost authority in the field of local advertising and marketing. Over the past thirty years, he and his partner, Dave Stilli, have held ownership or executive positions in retail, in advertising agencies, and in the media. This background gives them the rare advantage of having participated in and observed local advertising and marketing from all possible perspectives. Michael Corbett's fact-based, no-nonsense, mathematically-grounded system of advertising has produced remarkable growth for countless local businesses, in any economy, no matter how strong the national or local competition.

Corbett and Stilli provide advisory services for all members of the media, for ad agencies, and for local businesses of all sizes and types, nationwide.

"The 33 Ruthless Rules of Local Advertising" is the result of decades of collaborative effort.

200

For information about advisory services, phone
The Michael Corbett Company
561-744-2404

To order:
The 33 Ruthless Rules of Local Advertising
books ($14.95) or audio cassettes ($29.95),
call Pinnacle Books, Inc. at
(800) 285-3210

e-mail: pinbooks@worldnet.att.net